These thoughts have been complied to help you

reflect on God or start a

conversation as you sip your morning brew.

I hope you enjoy!

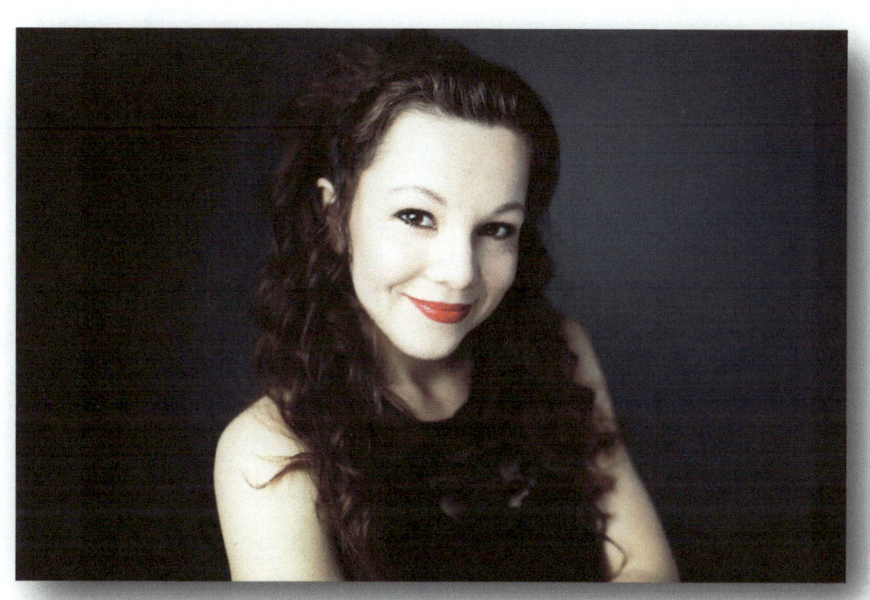

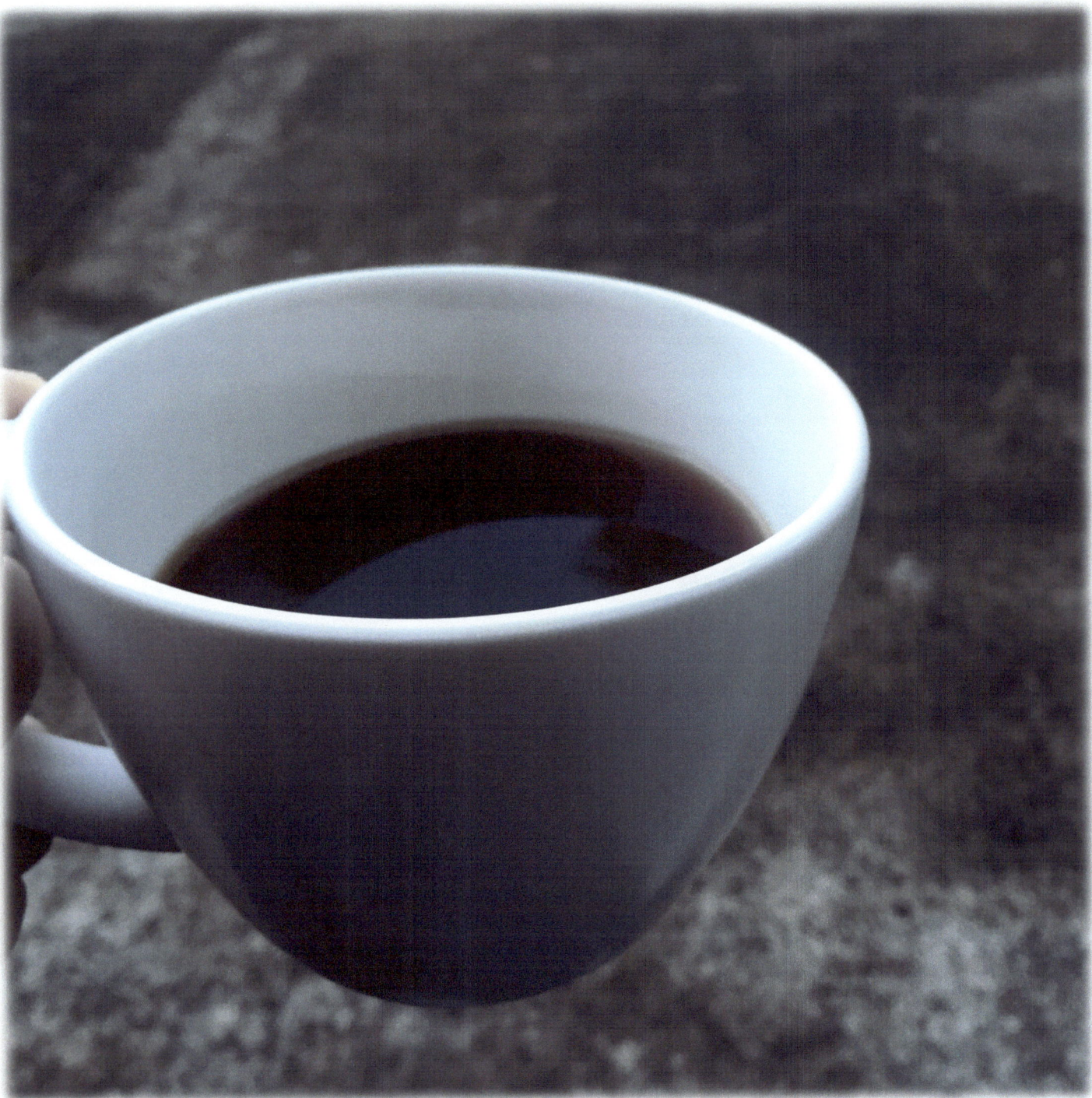

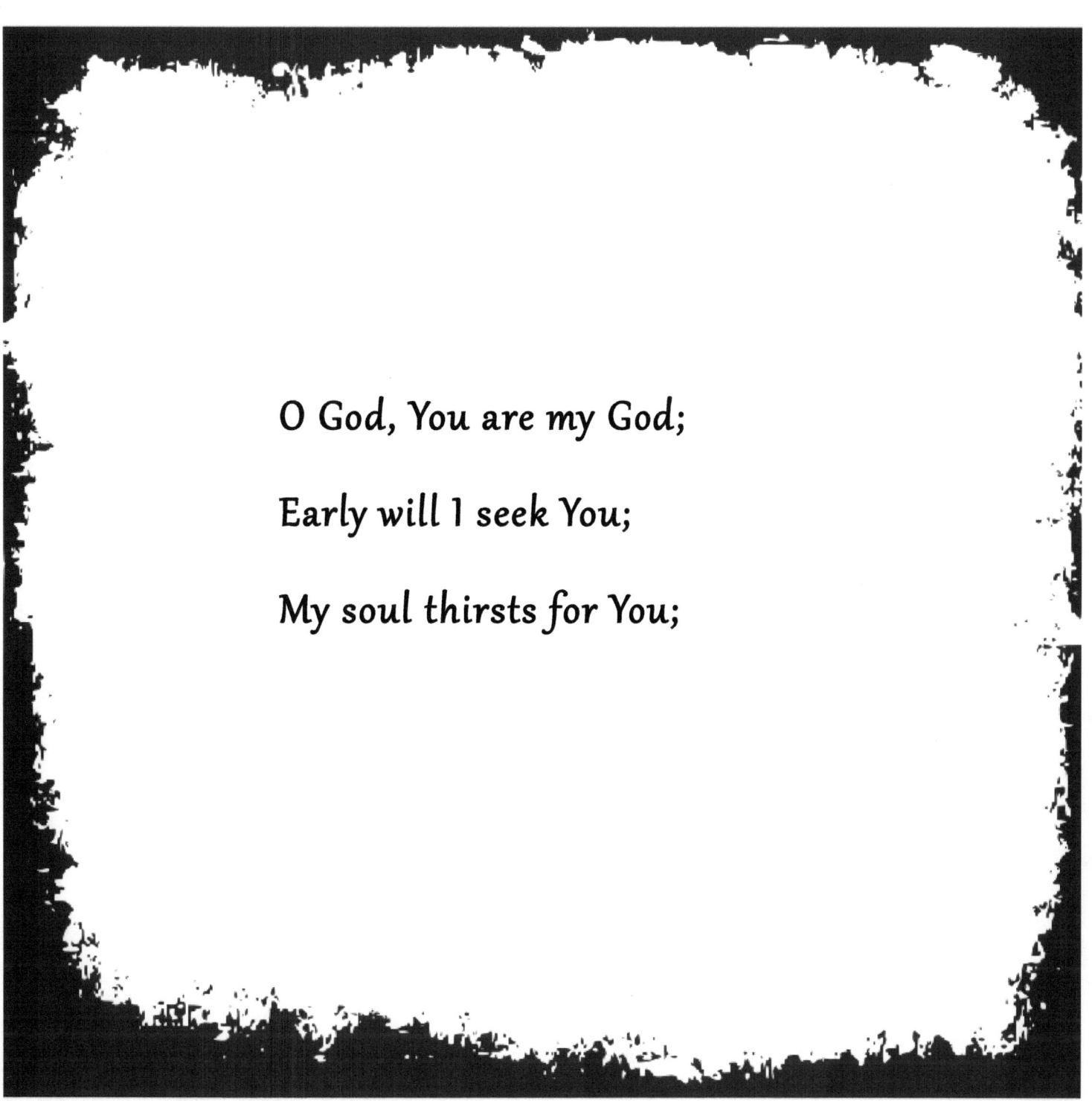

O God, You are my God;

Early will I seek You;

My soul thirsts for You;

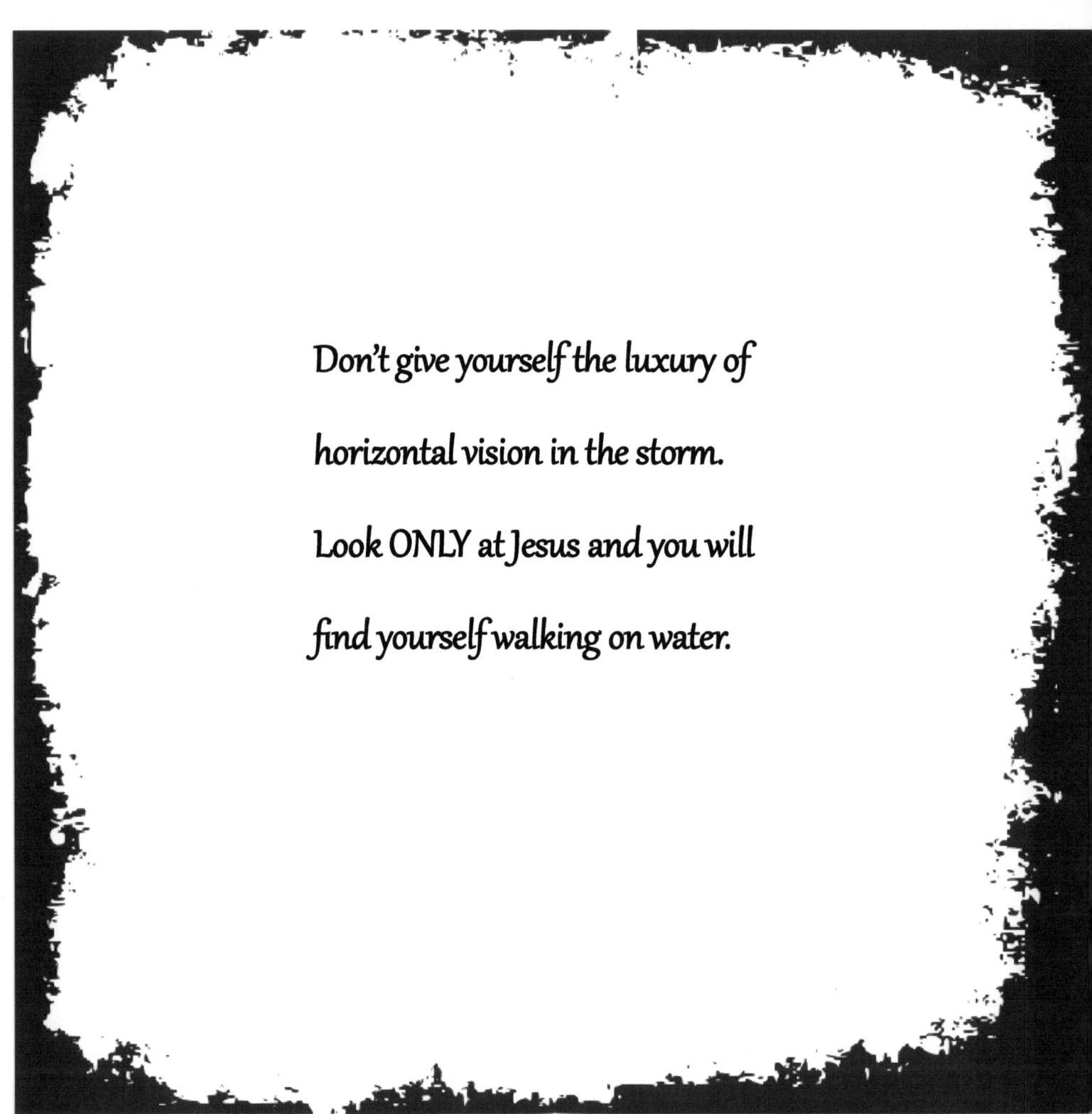

Don't give yourself the luxury of

horizontal vision in the storm.

Look ONLY at Jesus and you will

find yourself walking on water.

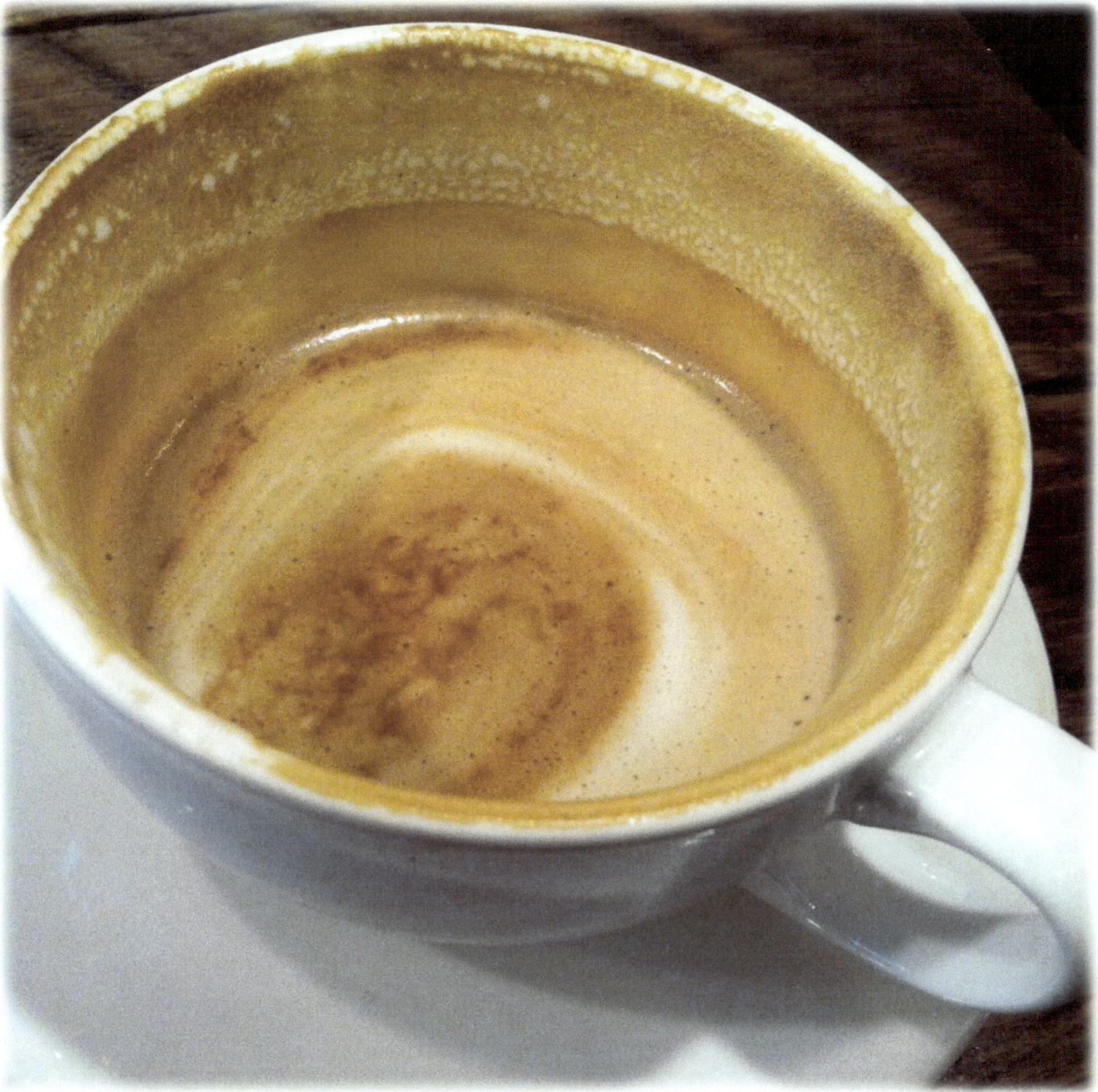

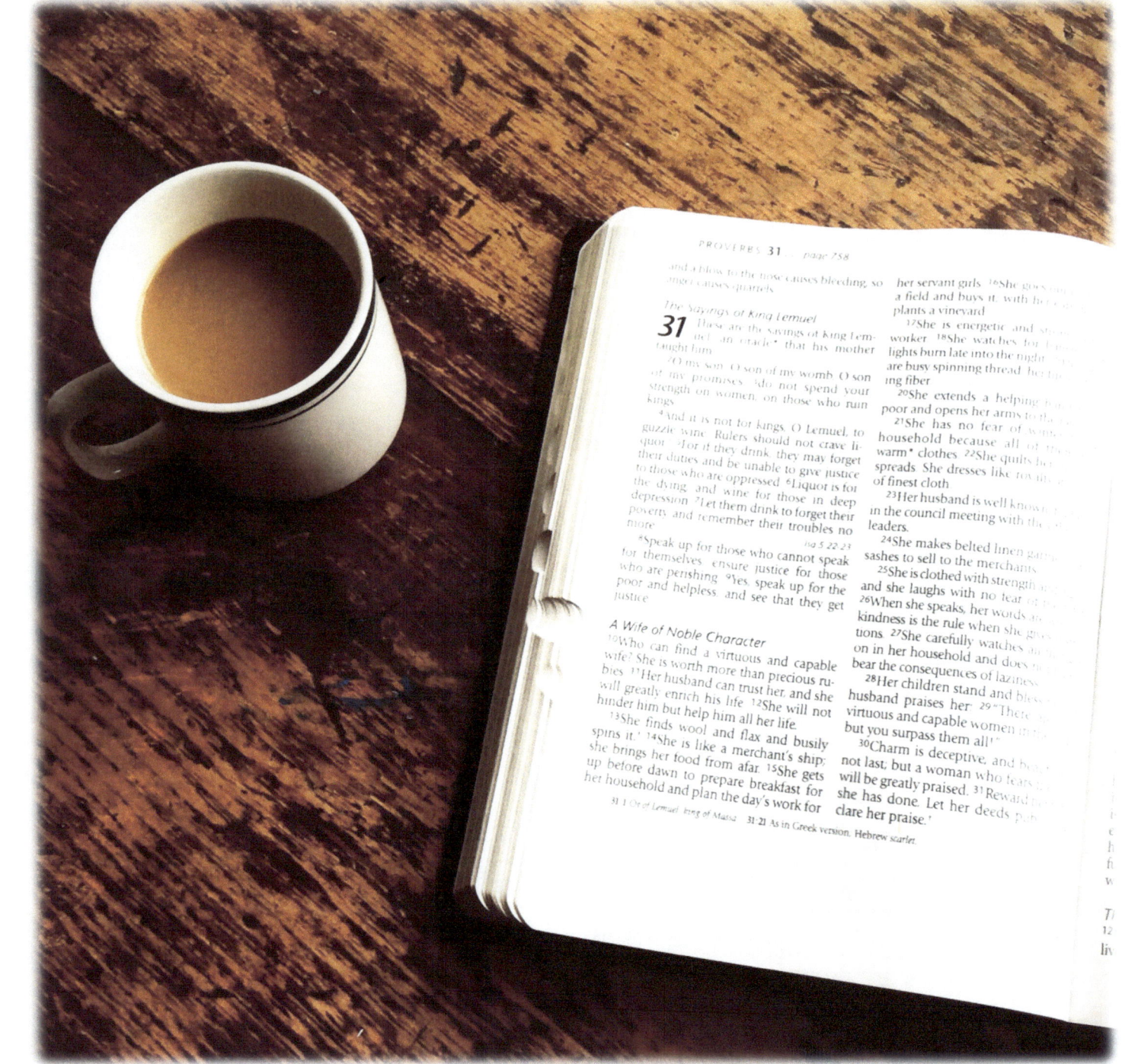

and a blow to the nose causes bleeding, so
anger causes quarrels.

The Sayings of King Lemuel

31 These are the sayings of King Lemuel, an oracle* that his mother
taught him:

²O my son, O son of my womb, O son
of my promises, ³do not spend your
strength on women, on those who ruin
kings.

⁴And it is not for kings, O Lemuel, to
guzzle wine. Rulers should not crave li-
quor. ⁵For if they drink, they may forget
their duties and be unable to give justice
to those who are oppressed. ⁶Liquor is for
the dying, and wine for those in deep
depression. ⁷Let them drink to forget their
poverty and remember their troubles no
more.

⁸Speak up for those who cannot speak
for themselves, ensure justice for those
who are perishing. ⁹Yes, speak up for the
poor and helpless, and see that they get
justice.

A Wife of Noble Character

¹⁰Who can find a virtuous and capable
wife? She is worth more than precious ru-
bies. ¹¹Her husband can trust her, and she
will greatly enrich his life. ¹²She will not
hinder him but help him all her life.

¹³She finds wool and flax and busily
spins it. ¹⁴She is like a merchant's ship;
she brings her food from afar. ¹⁵She gets
up before dawn to prepare breakfast for
her household and plan the day's work for

her servant girls. ¹⁶She goes out to inspect
a field and buys it; with her earnings she
plants a vineyard.

¹⁷She is energetic and strong, a hard
worker. ¹⁸She watches for bargains; her
lights burn late into the night. ¹⁹Her hands
are busy spinning thread, her fingers twist-
ing fiber.

²⁰She extends a helping hand to the
poor and opens her arms to the needy.

²¹She has no fear of winter for her
household, because all of them have
warm* clothes. ²²She quilts her own bed-
spreads. She dresses like royalty in gowns
of finest cloth.

²³Her husband is well known, for he sits
in the council meeting with the other civic
leaders.

²⁴She makes belted linen garments and
sashes to sell to the merchants.

²⁵She is clothed with strength and dignity,
and she laughs with no fear of the future.
²⁶When she speaks, her words are wise, and
kindness is the rule when she gives instruc-
tions. ²⁷She carefully watches all that goes
on in her household and does not have to
bear the consequences of laziness.

²⁸Her children stand and bless her. Her
husband praises her: ²⁹"There are many
virtuous and capable women in the world,
but you surpass them all!"

³⁰Charm is deceptive, and beauty does
not last; but a woman who fears the LORD
will be greatly praised. ³¹Reward her for all
she has done. Let her deeds publicly de-
clare her praise.'

31:1 Or of Lemuel, king of Massa.   31:21 As in Greek version. Hebrew scarlet.

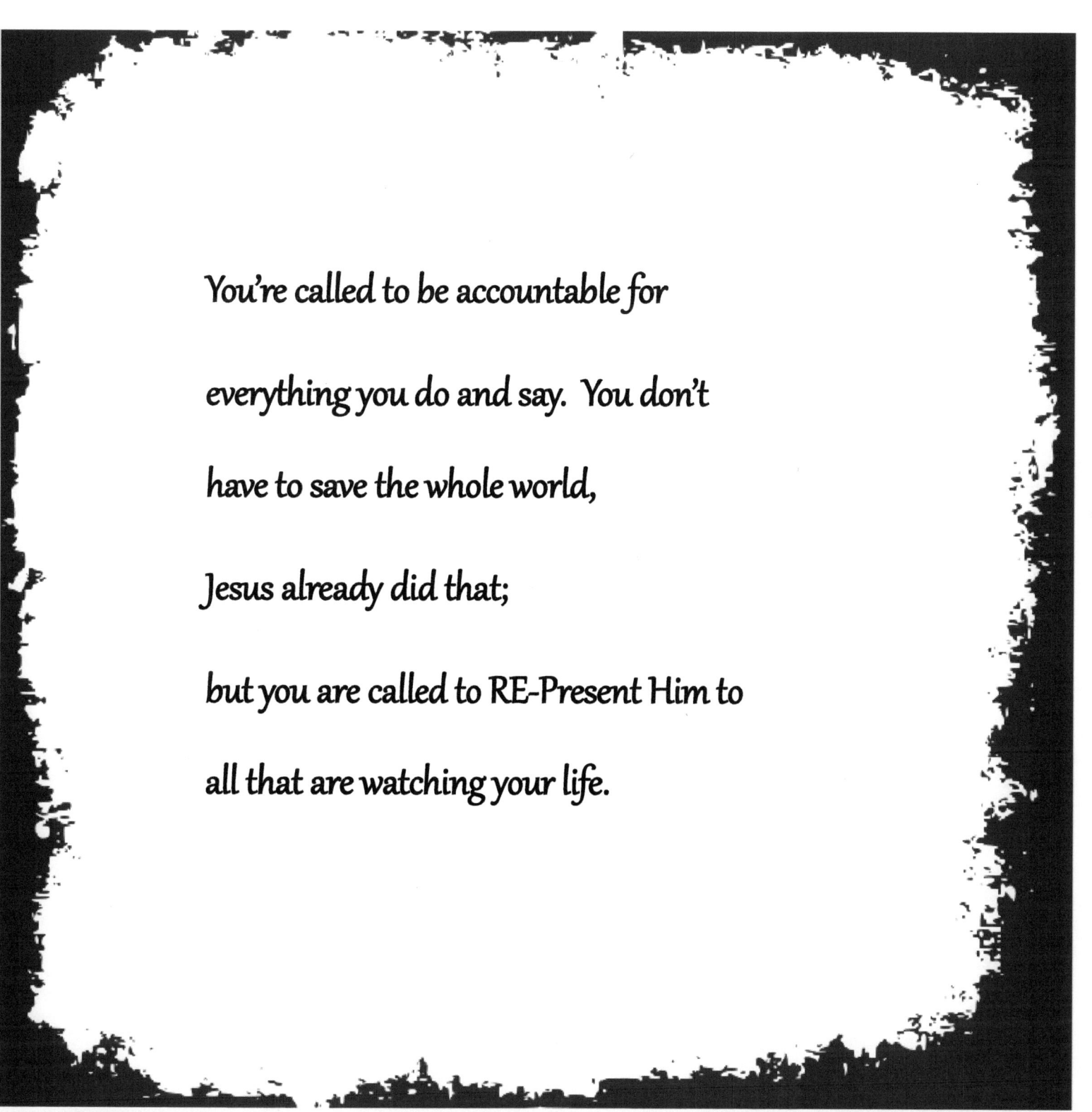

You're called to be accountable for

everything you do and say. You don't

have to save the whole world,

Jesus already did that;

but you are called to RE-Present Him to

all that are watching your life.

What if everything gets dark

and you feel like everything is breaking,

changing or closing in around you?

You feel buried, but what if,

you've been planted.

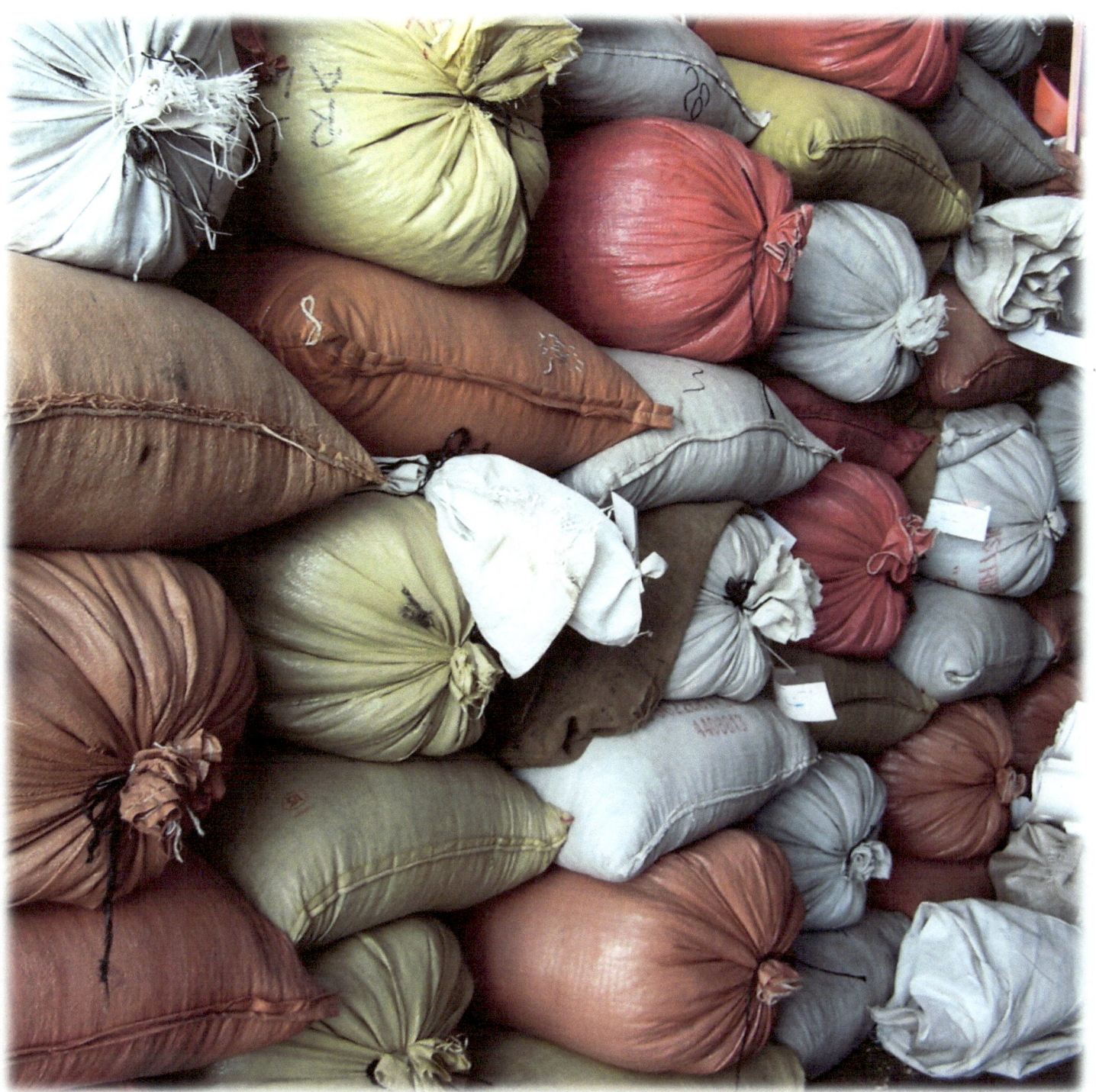

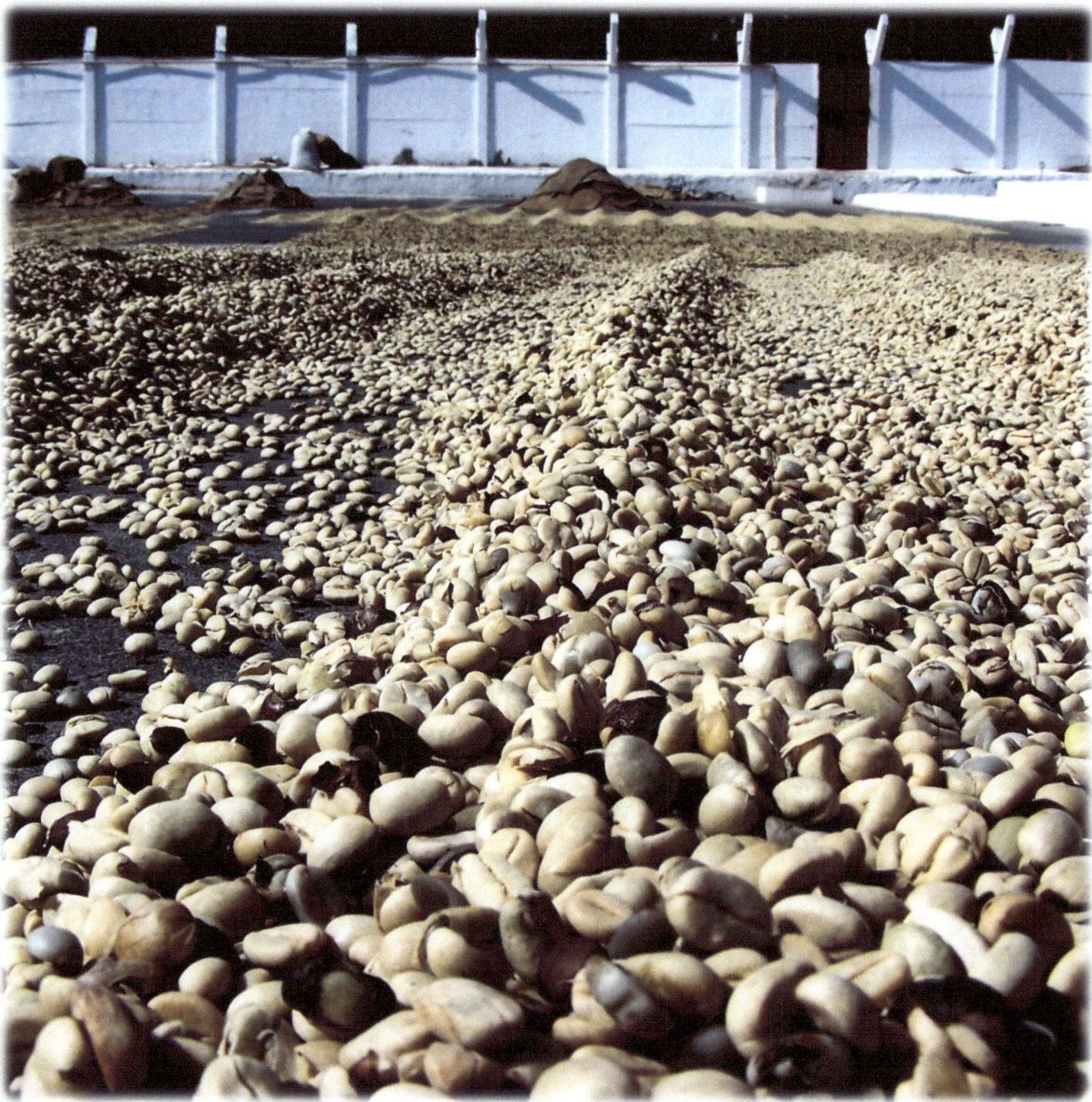

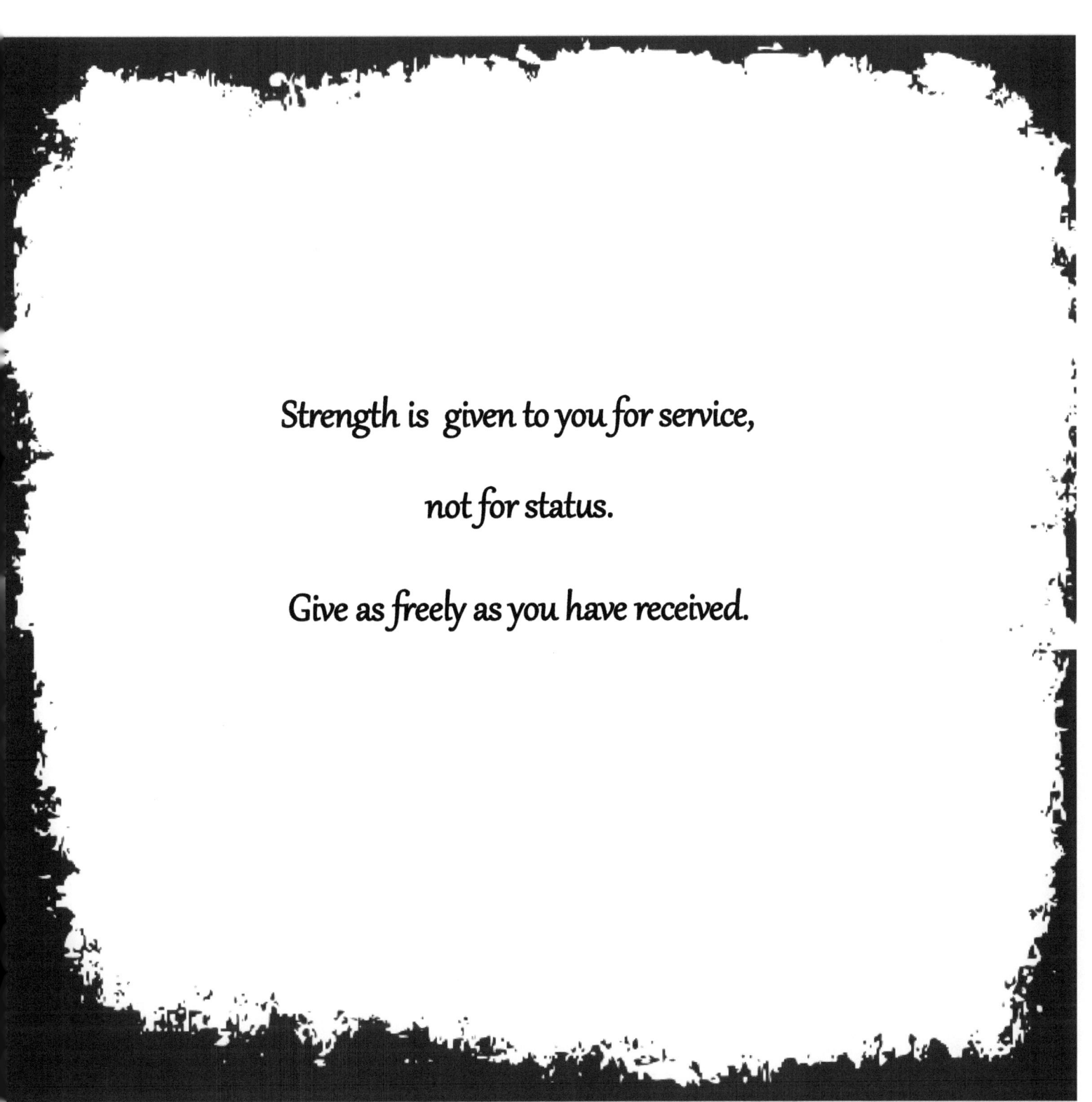

Strength is given to you for service,

not for status.

Give as freely as you have received.

A growing knowledge of God

displaces the fear of people.

When you see God for who he is,

you fear him. And when you

fear God, you fear nothing else.

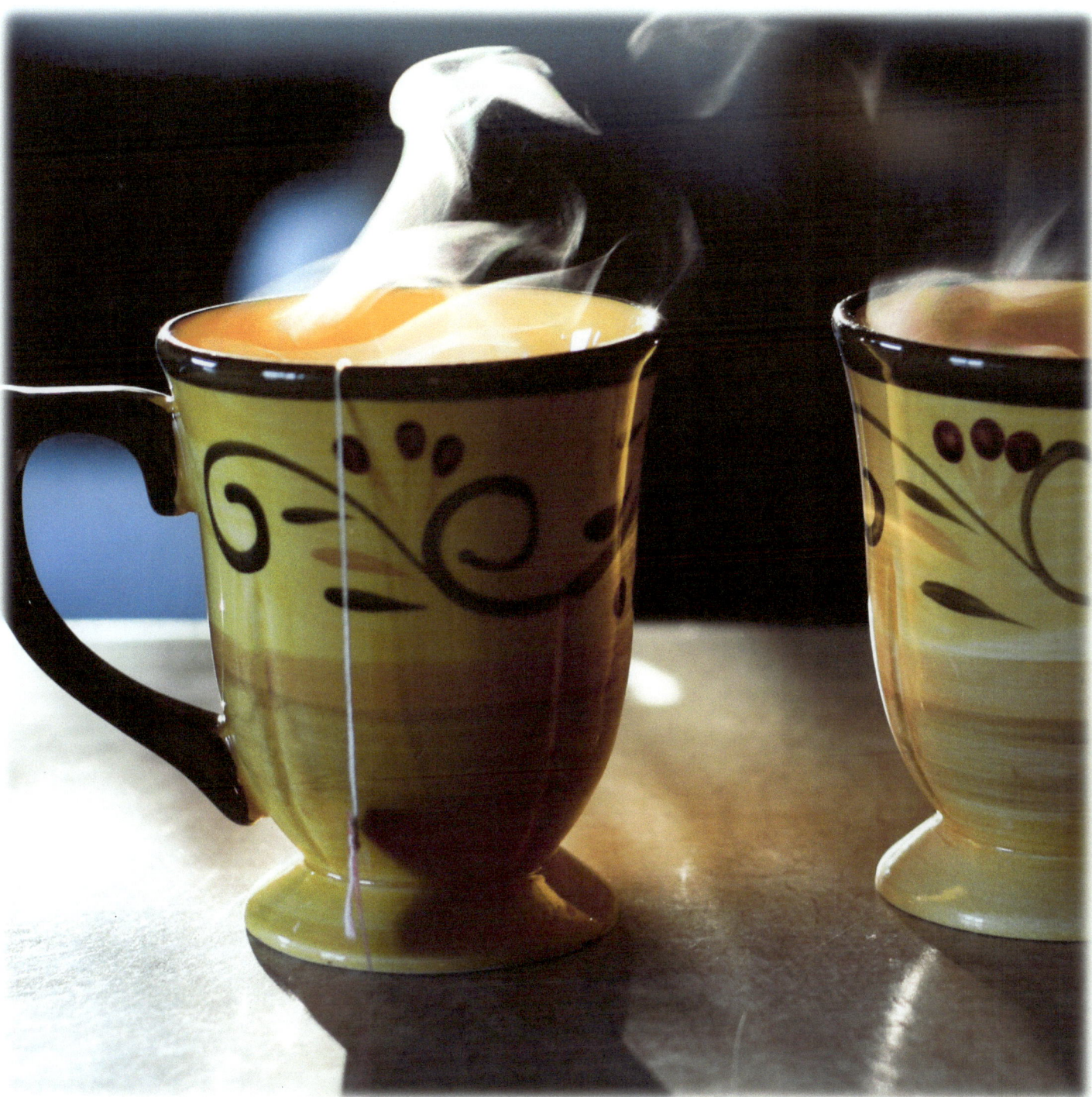

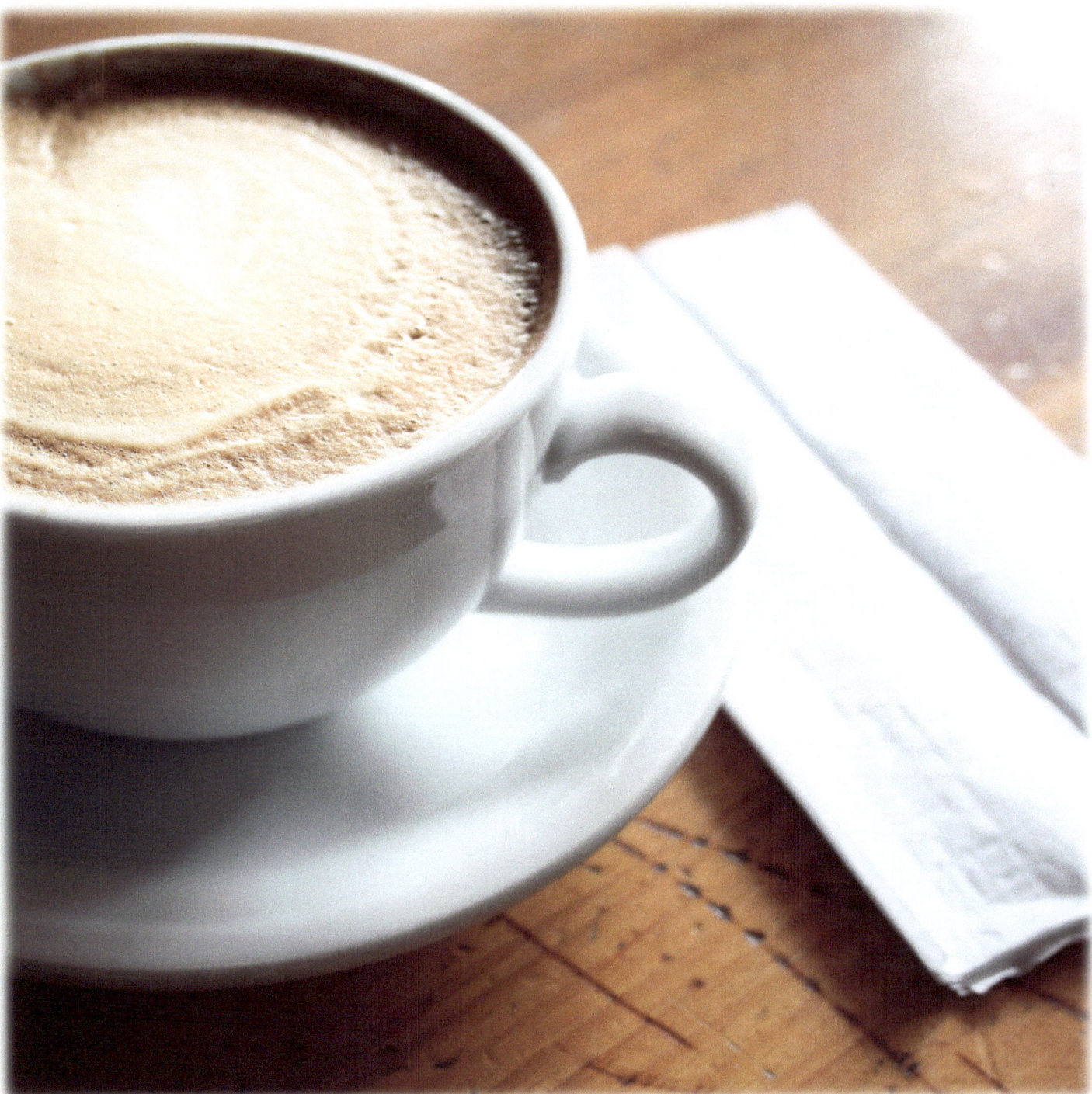

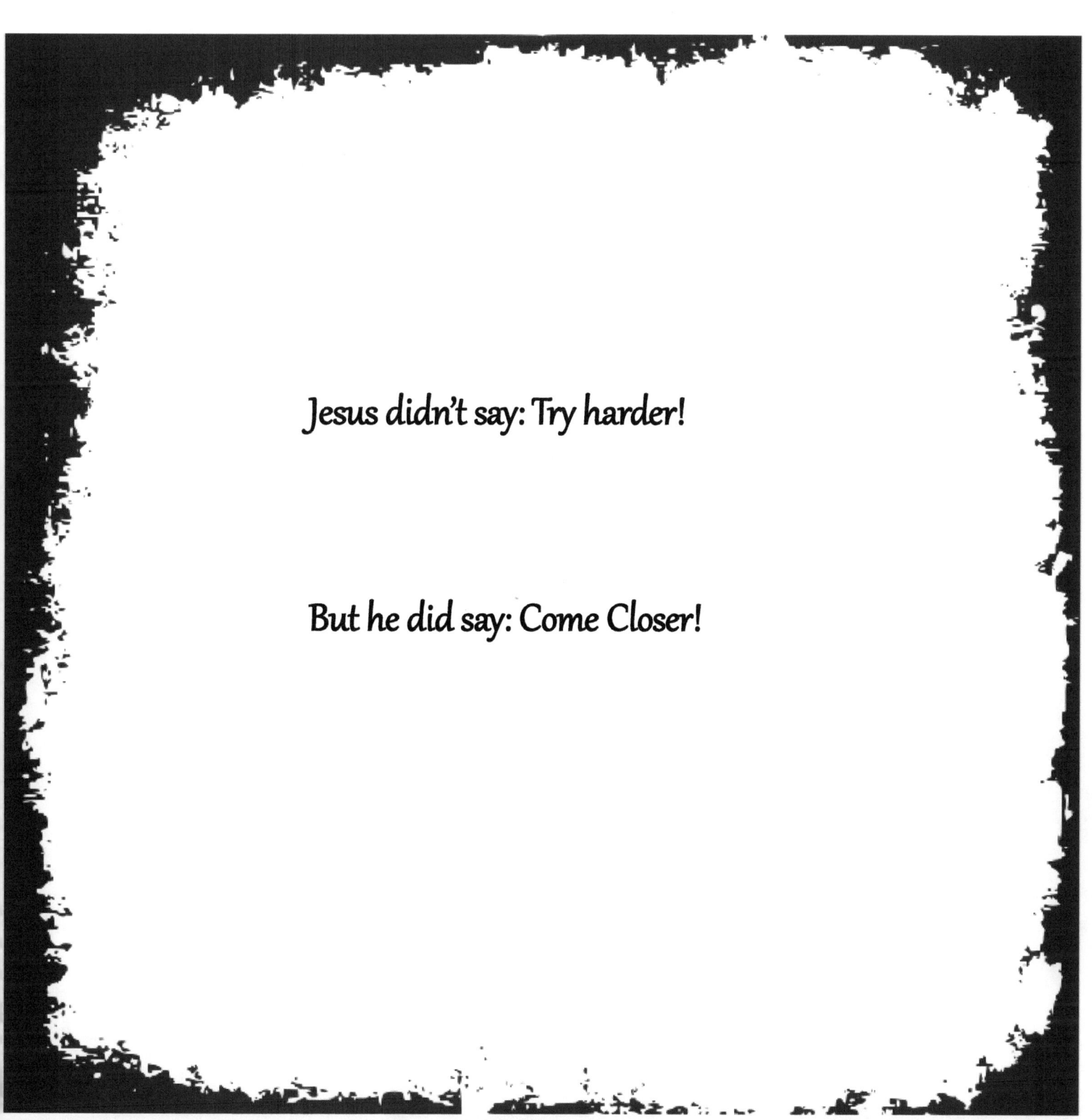

Jesus didn't say: Try harder!

But he did say: Come Closer!

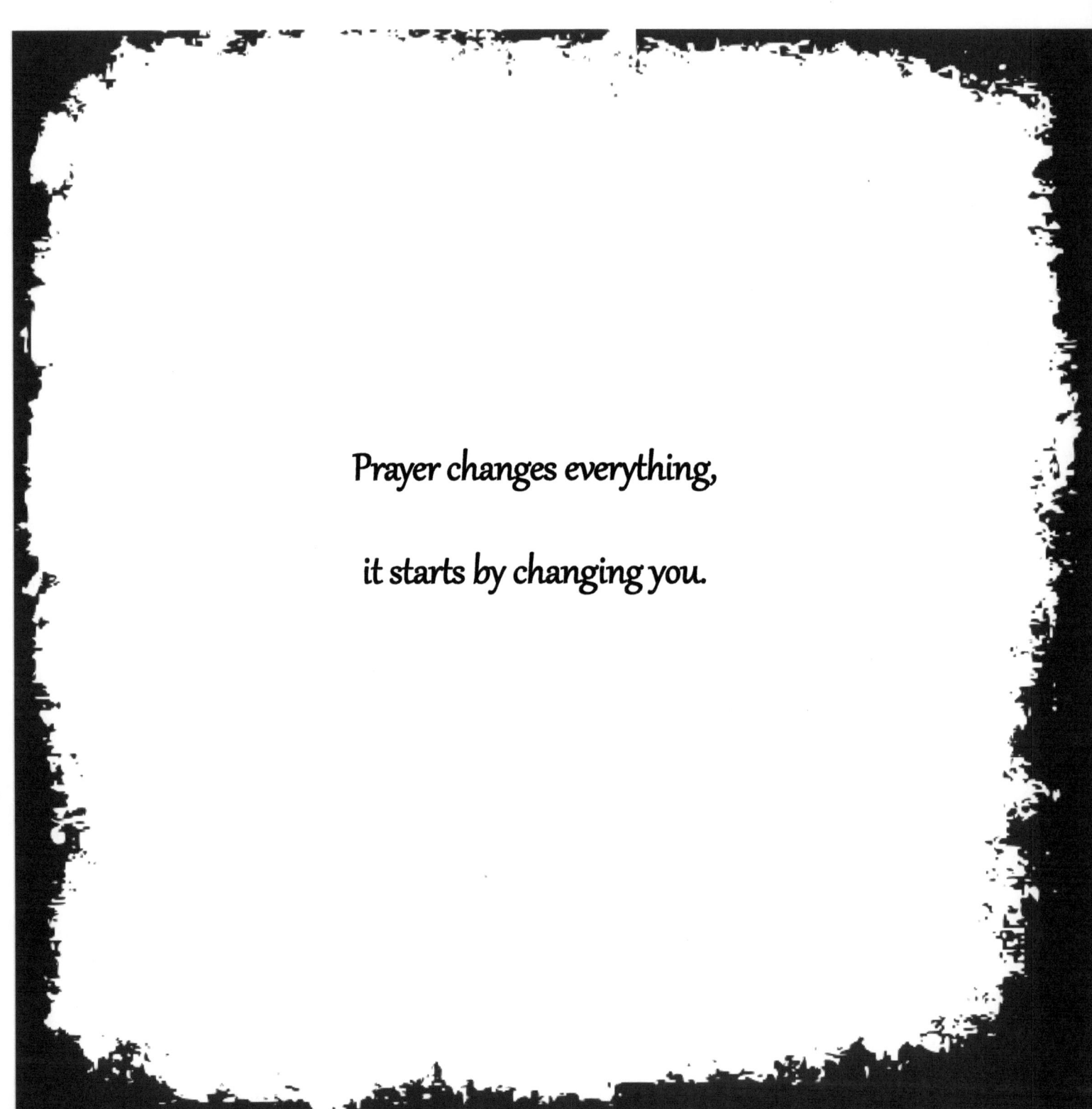

Prayer changes everything,

it starts by changing you.

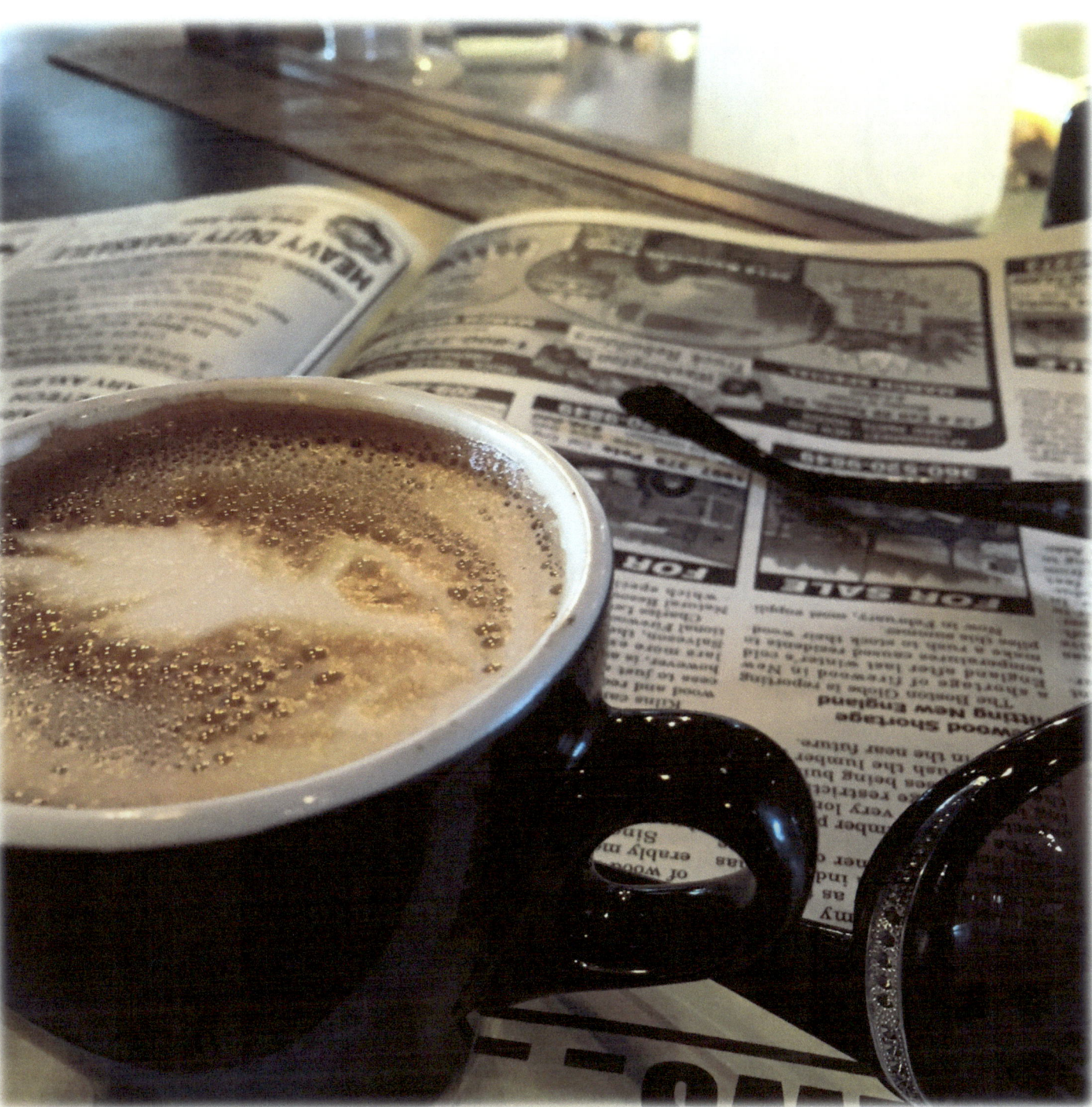

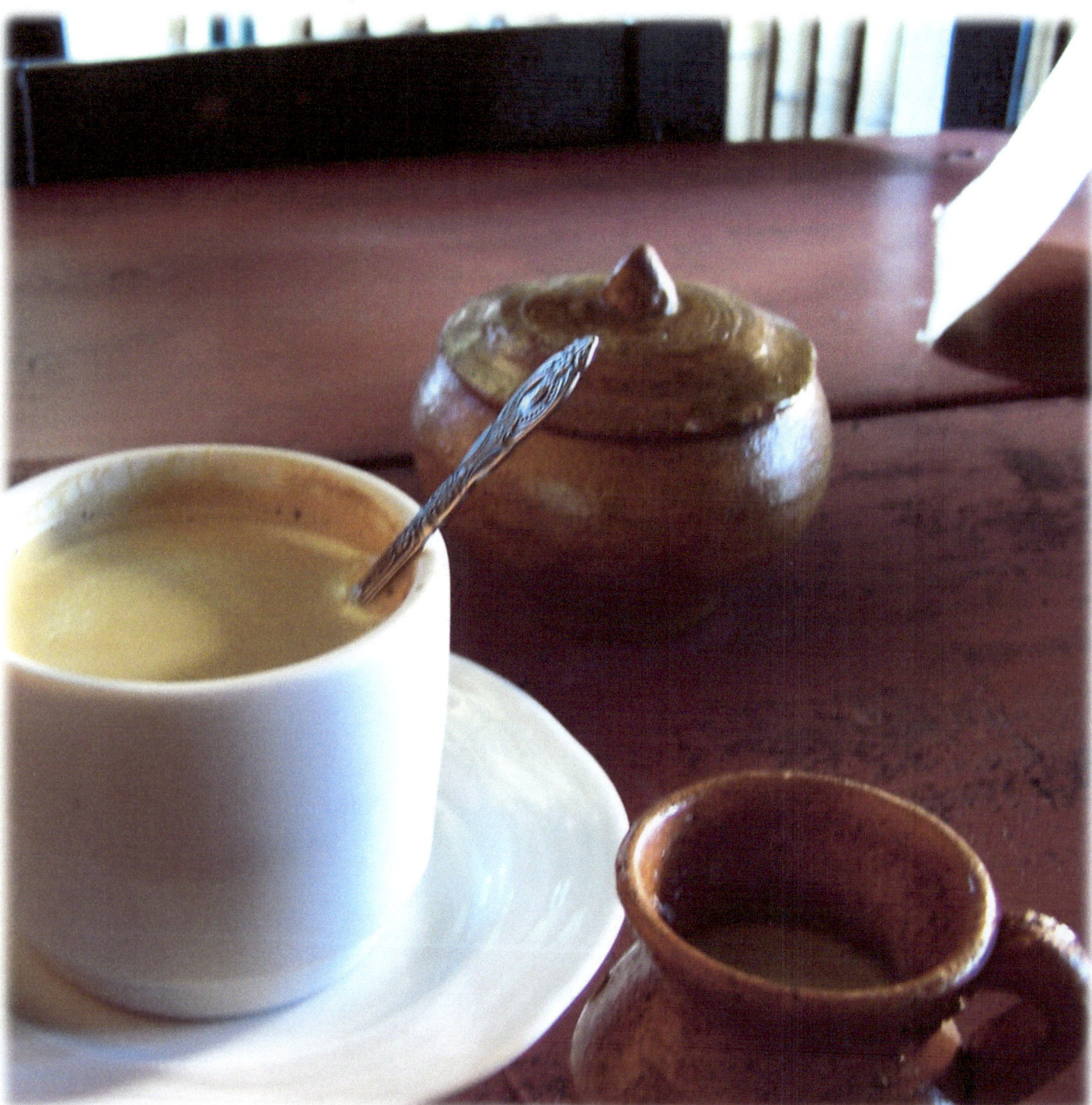

A child believes. A child doesn't overthink

but trusts with their heart. A child knows

Papa. God has called us his dearly loved

children, let's act like it!

God looks at your sin and very simply

replies: "Yes, I still love you! I never

stopped and I never will! Now, let's deal

with your sin together."

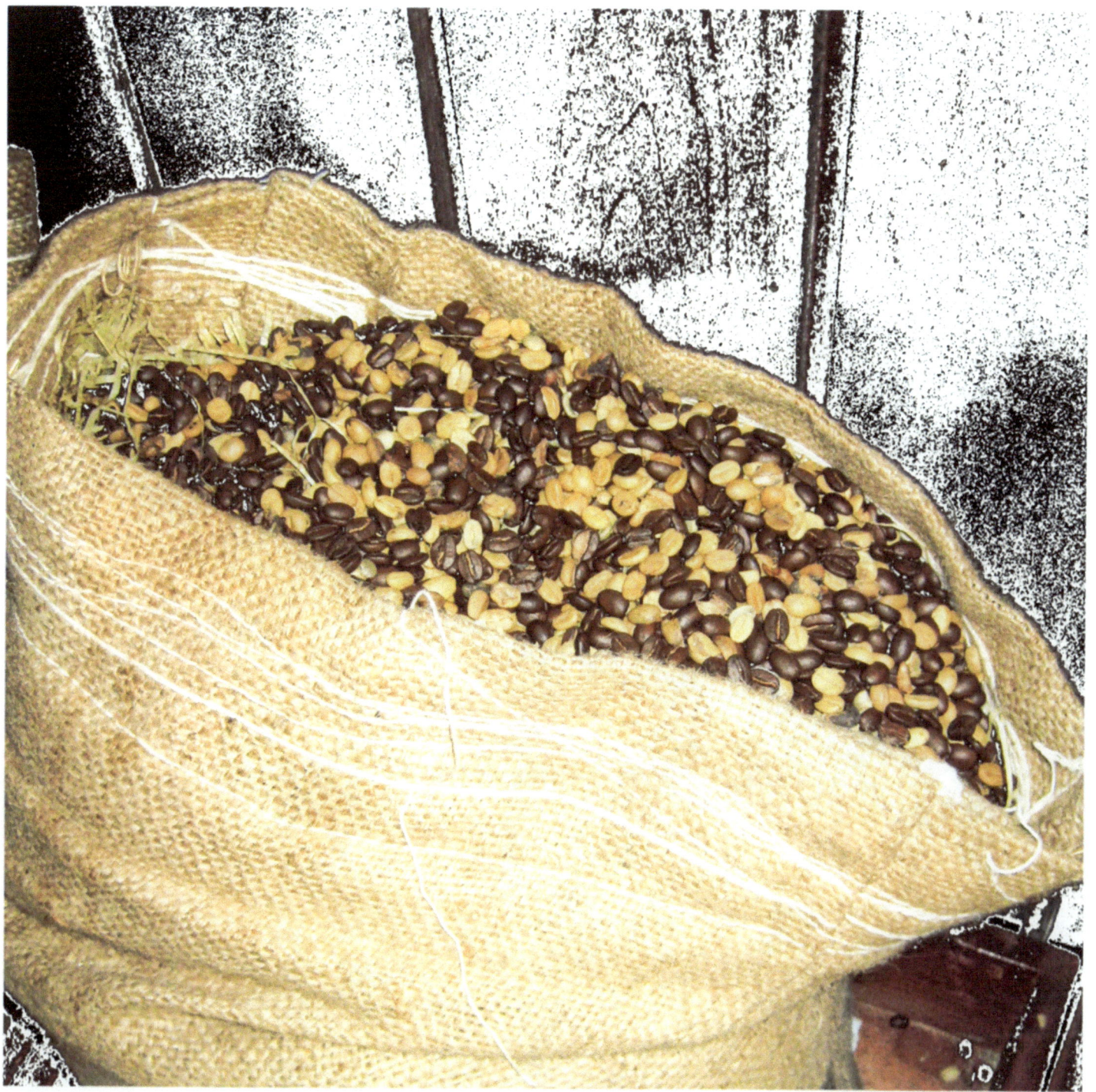

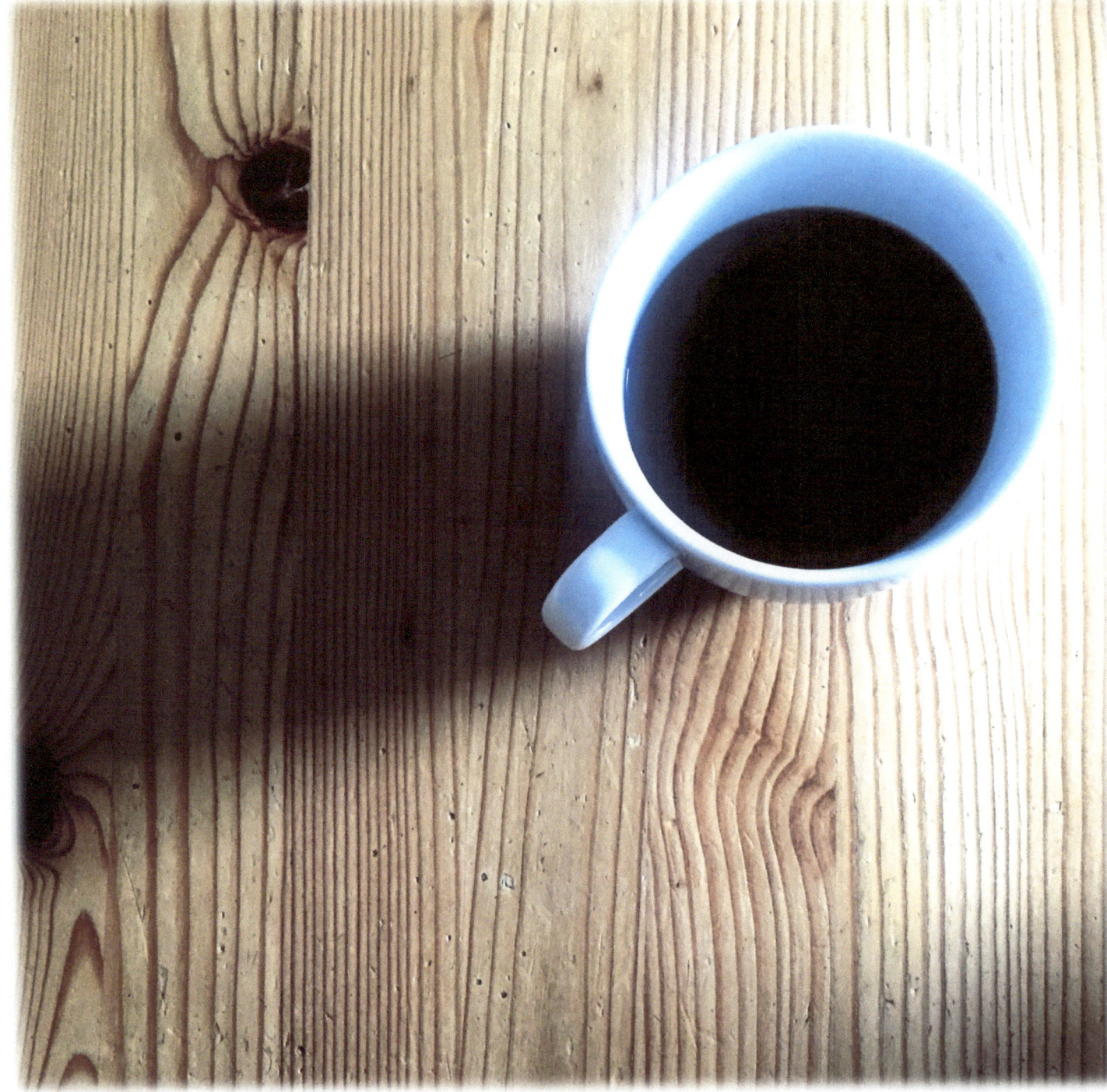

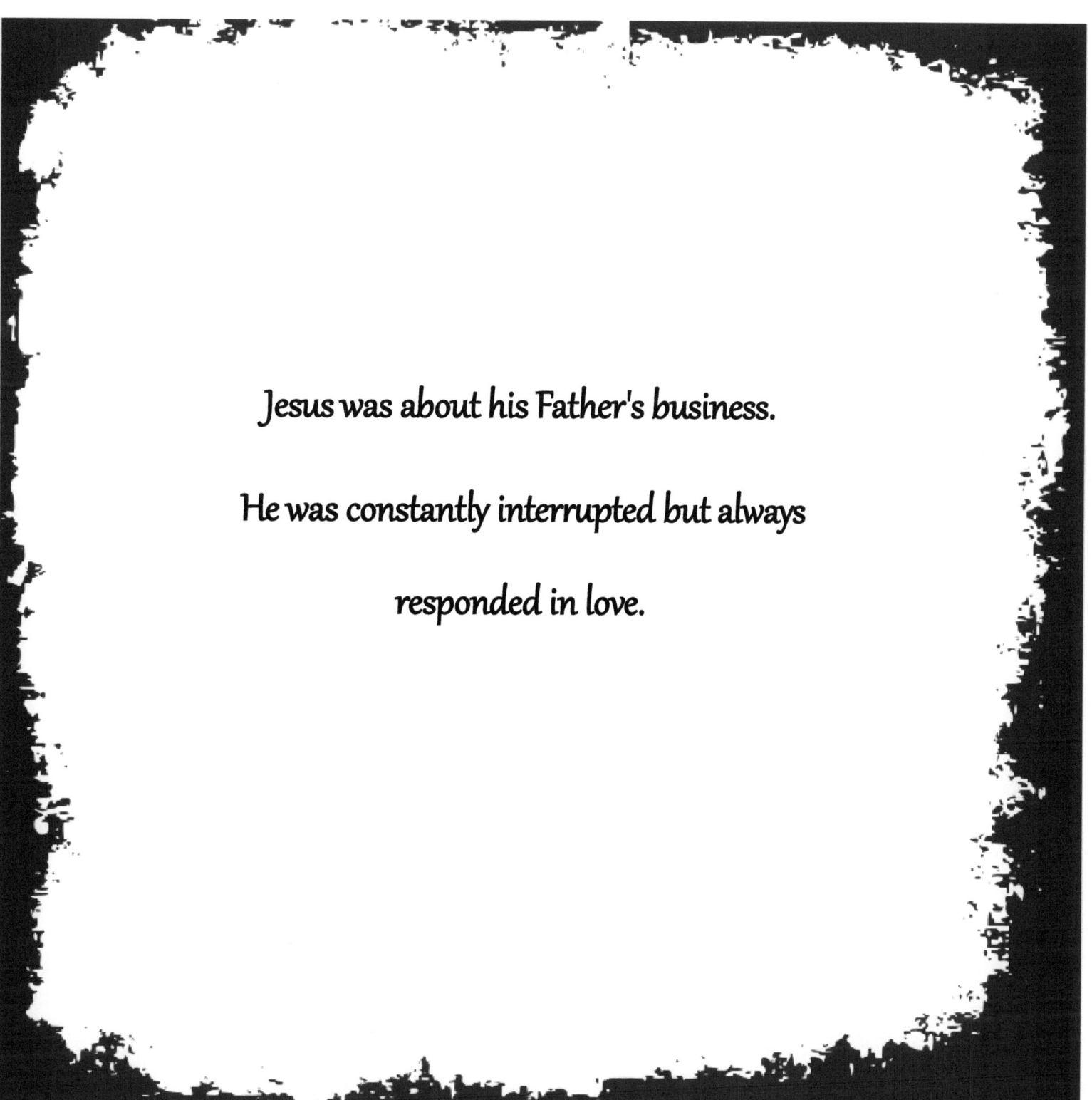

Jesus was about his Father's business.

He was constantly interrupted but always

responded in love.

God said to seek him with my whole heart.

I reach about 90% on my own but when

pain and suffering come into my life, I reach

100% out of desperation.

God uses everything.

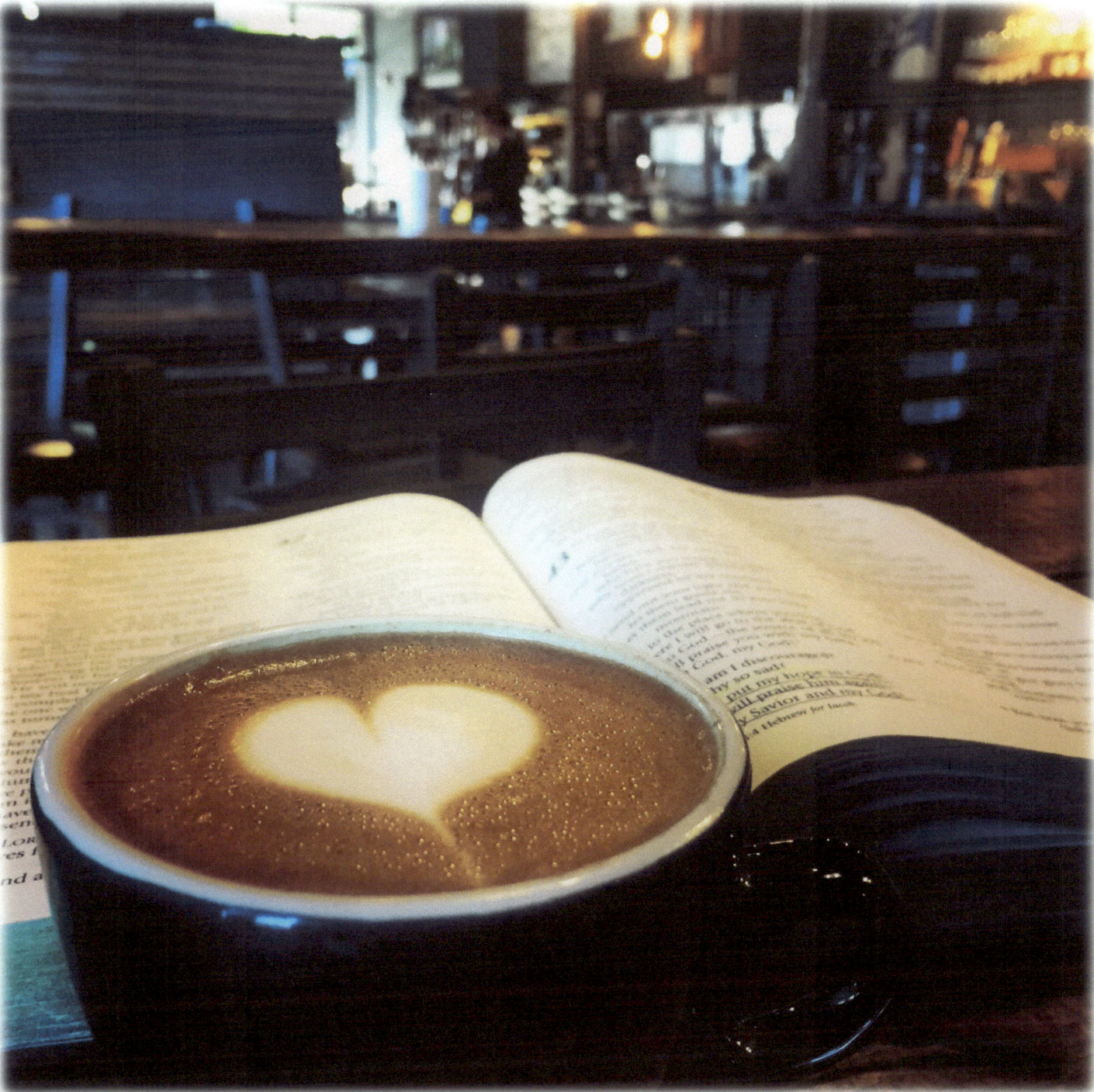

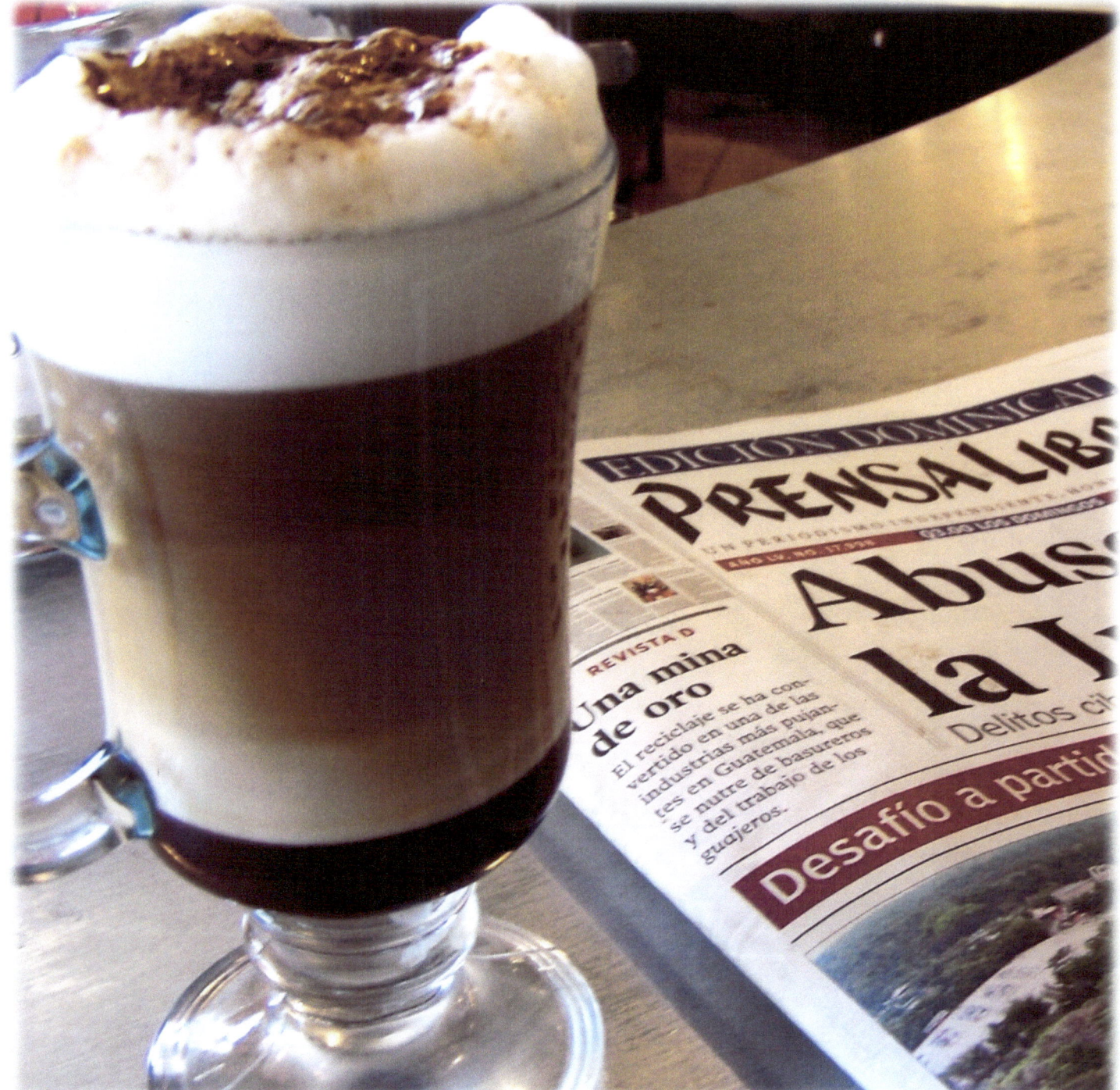

How do you see yourself?

How do you think God sees you?

When Jesus paid for your freedom,

he also gave you a robe of

righteousness. When God looks at

you, he sees that righteousness.

I know you.

I care about you.

I've got you safe.

Trust me, know I am God, be still.

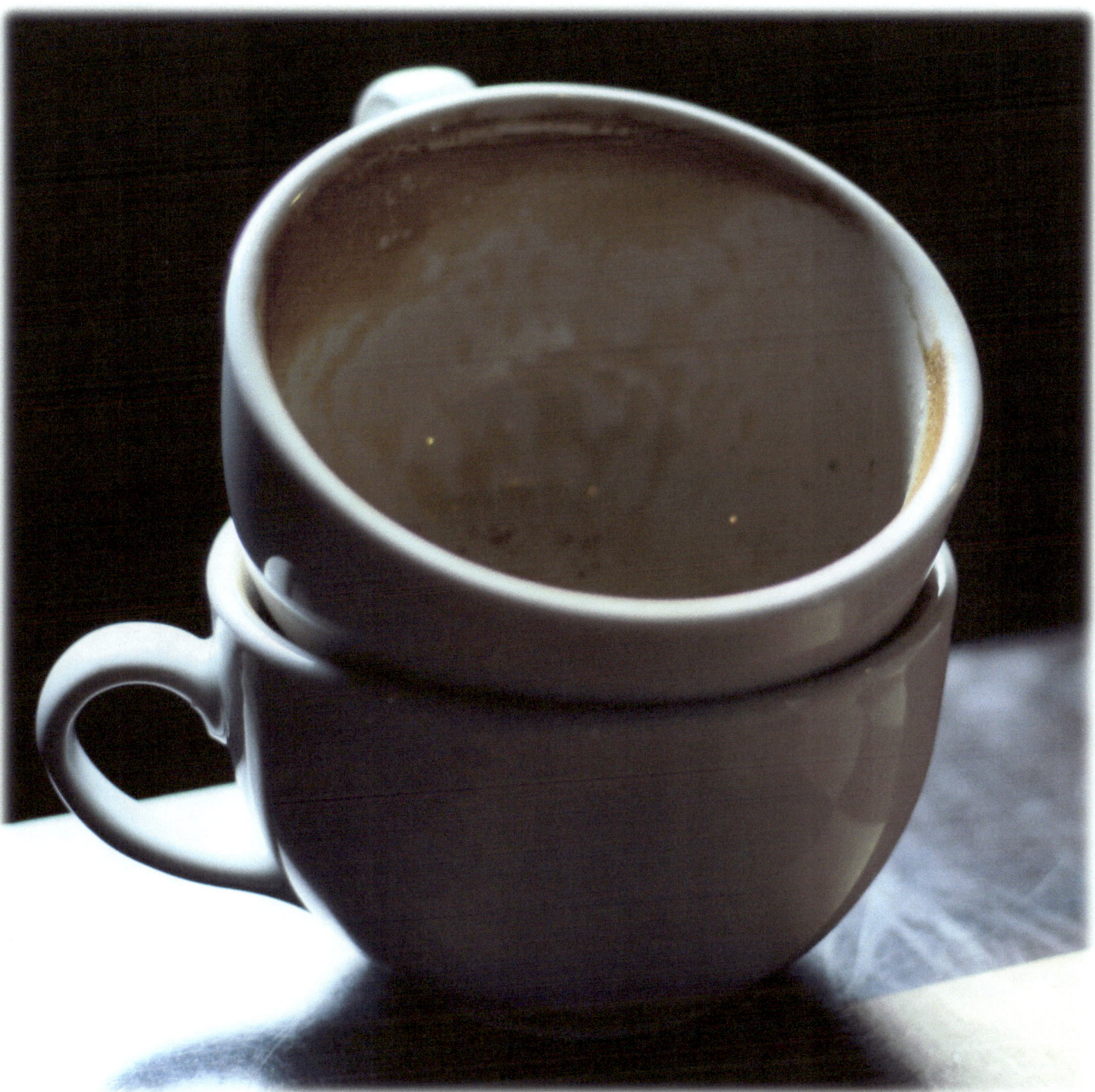

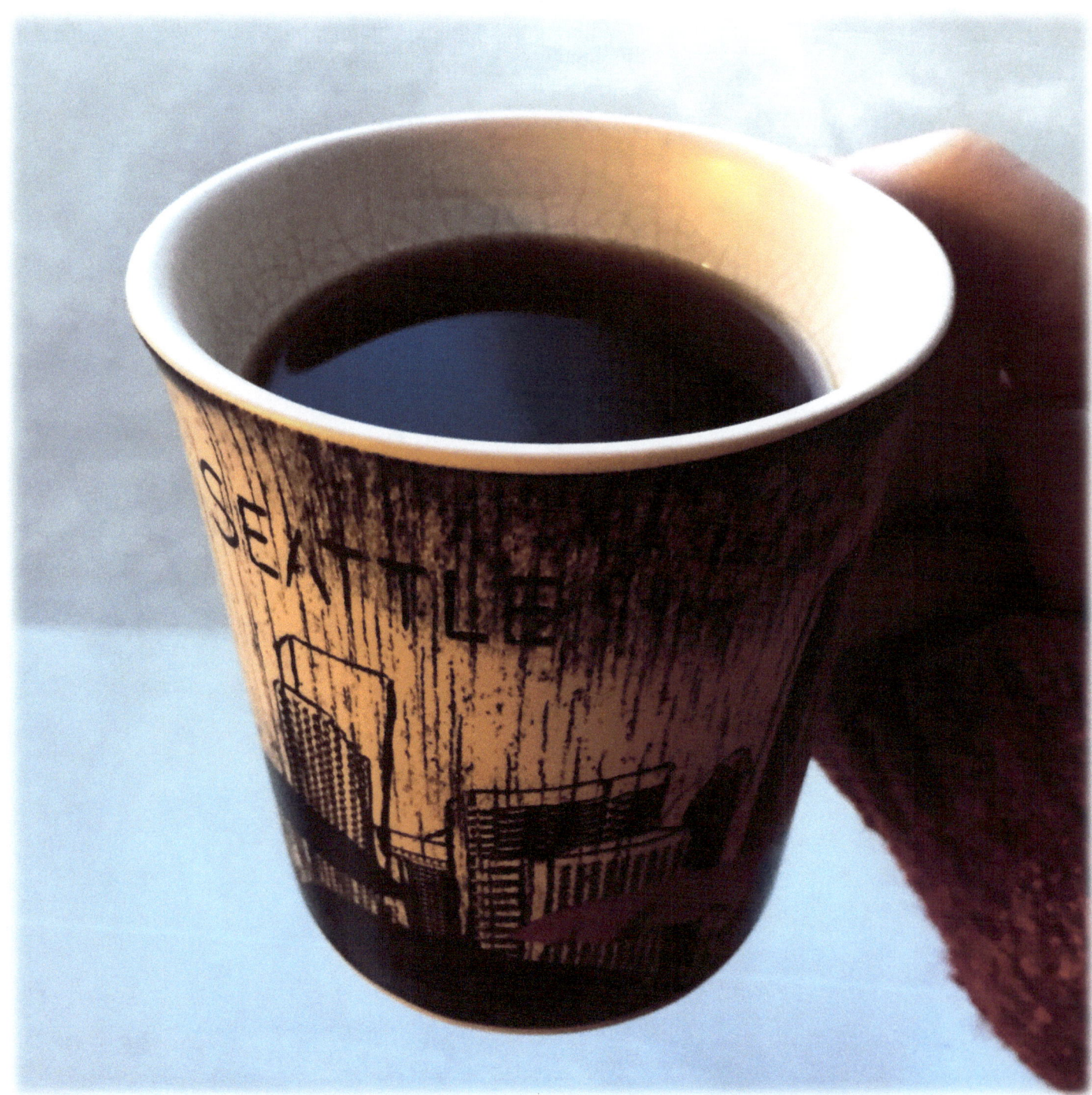

If you can make your

dreams come true without

God's help then it's time to

dream BIGGER!

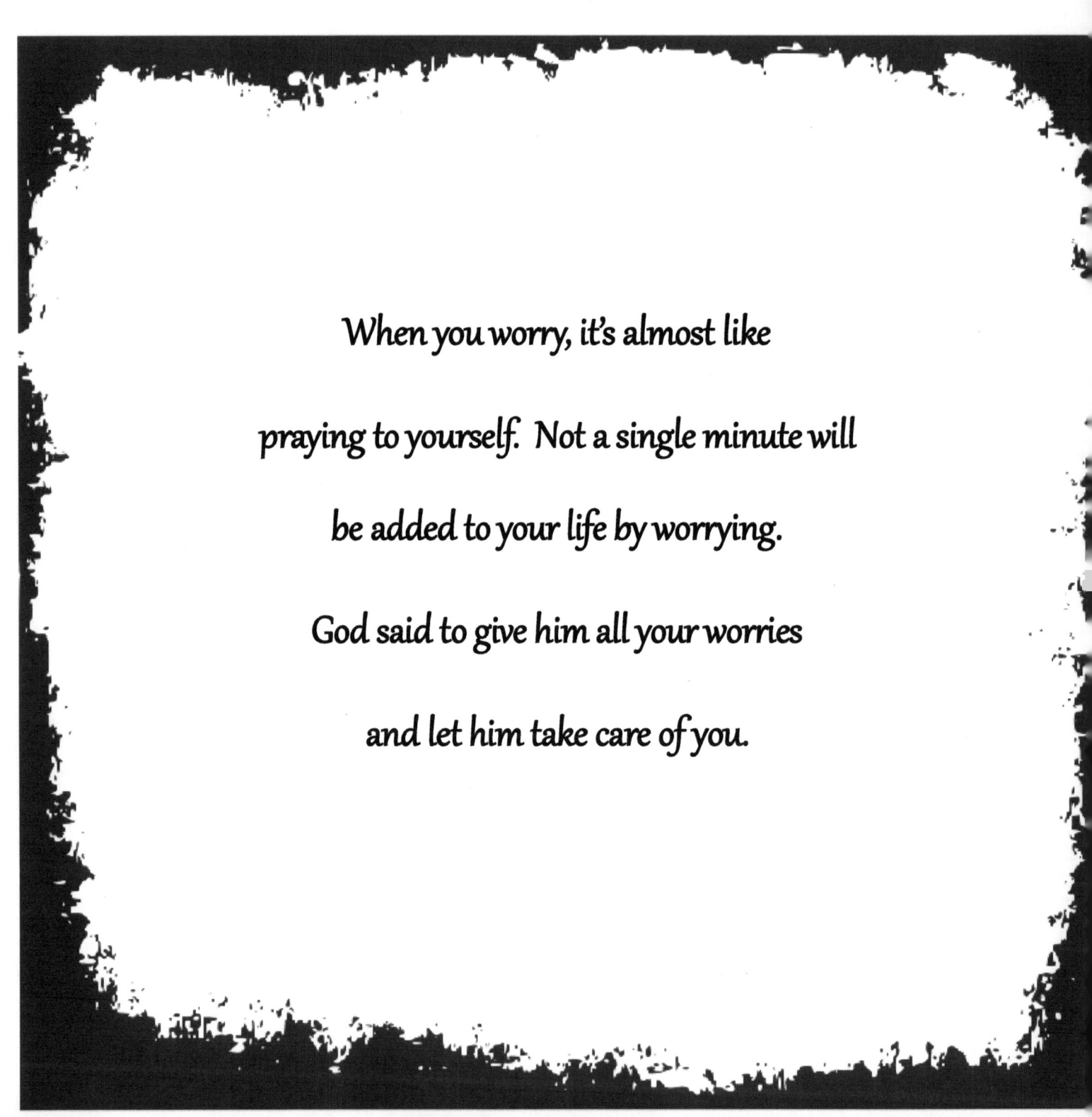

When you worry, it's almost like

praying to yourself. Not a single minute will

be added to your life by worrying.

God said to give him all your worries

and let him take care of you.

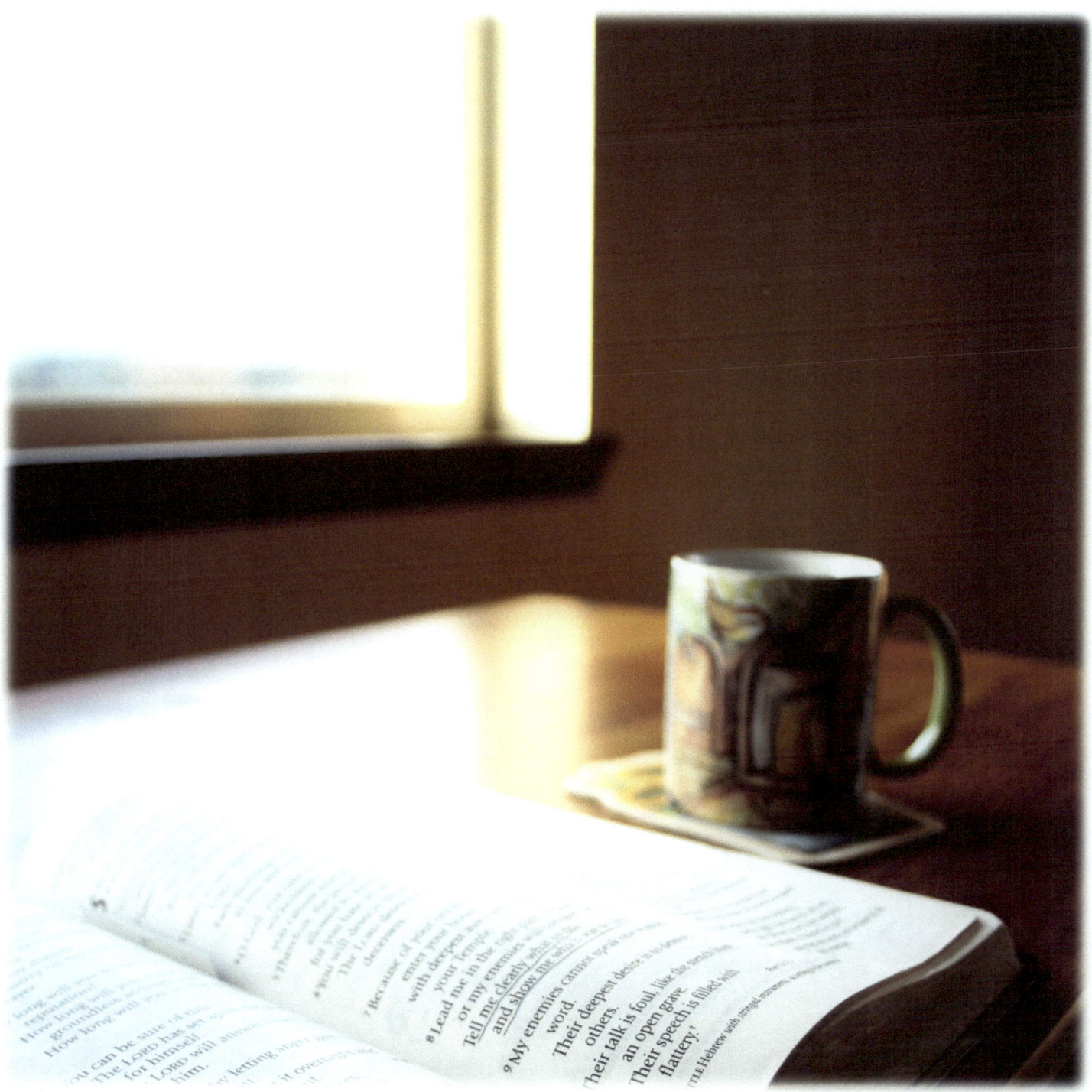

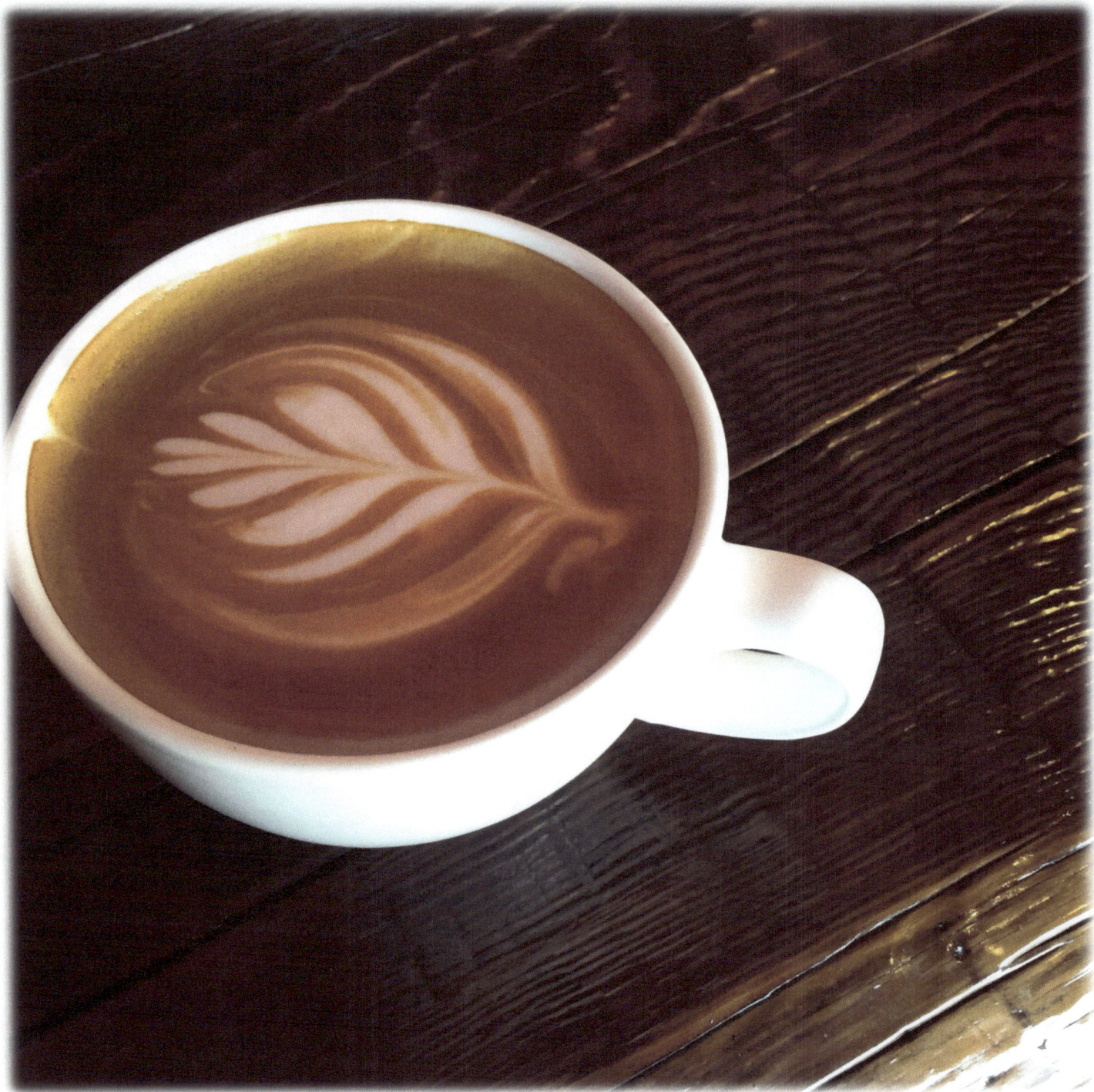

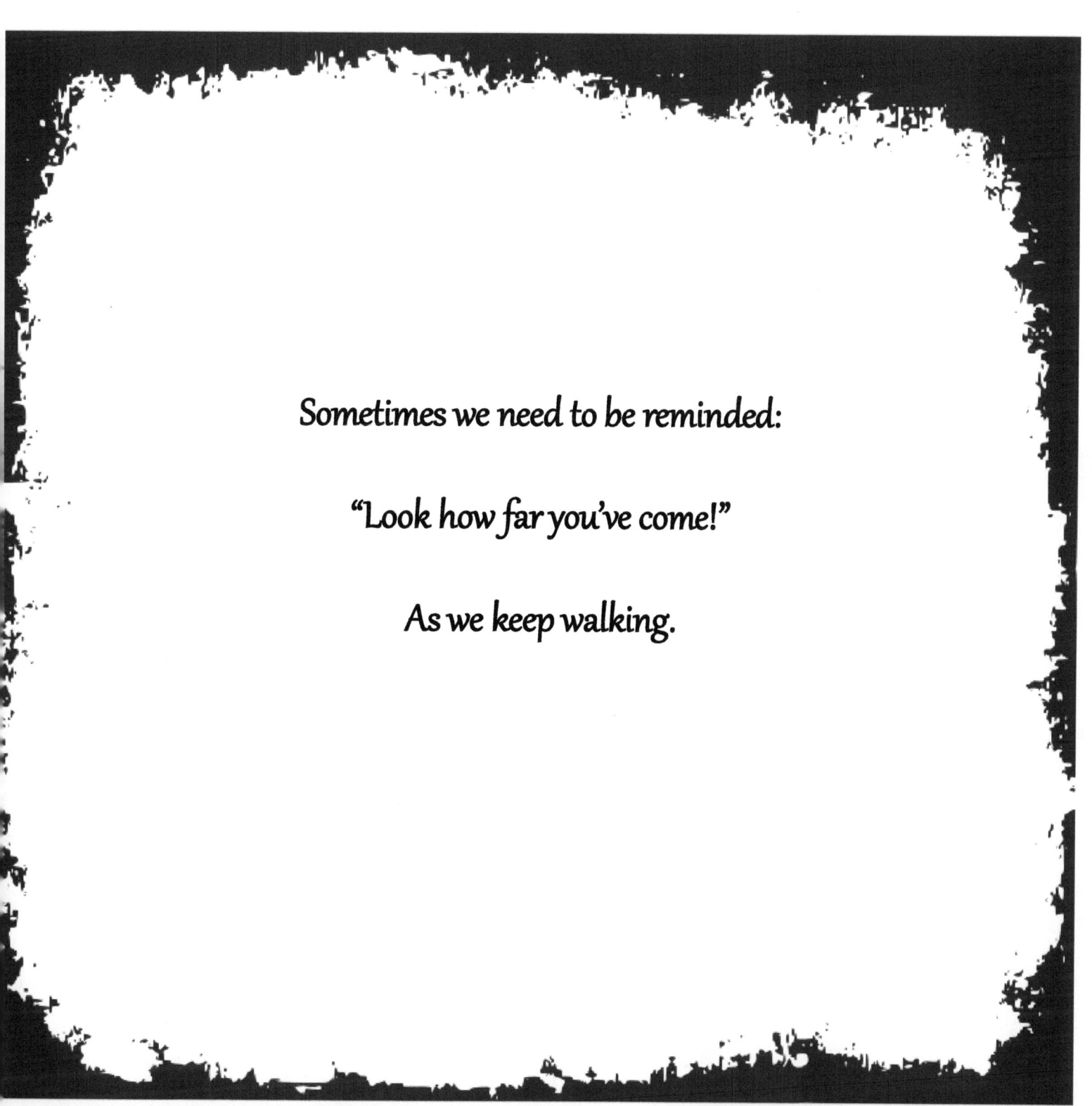

Sometimes we need to be reminded:

"Look how far you've come!"

As we keep walking.

When you praise God,

You bring problems to your problems.

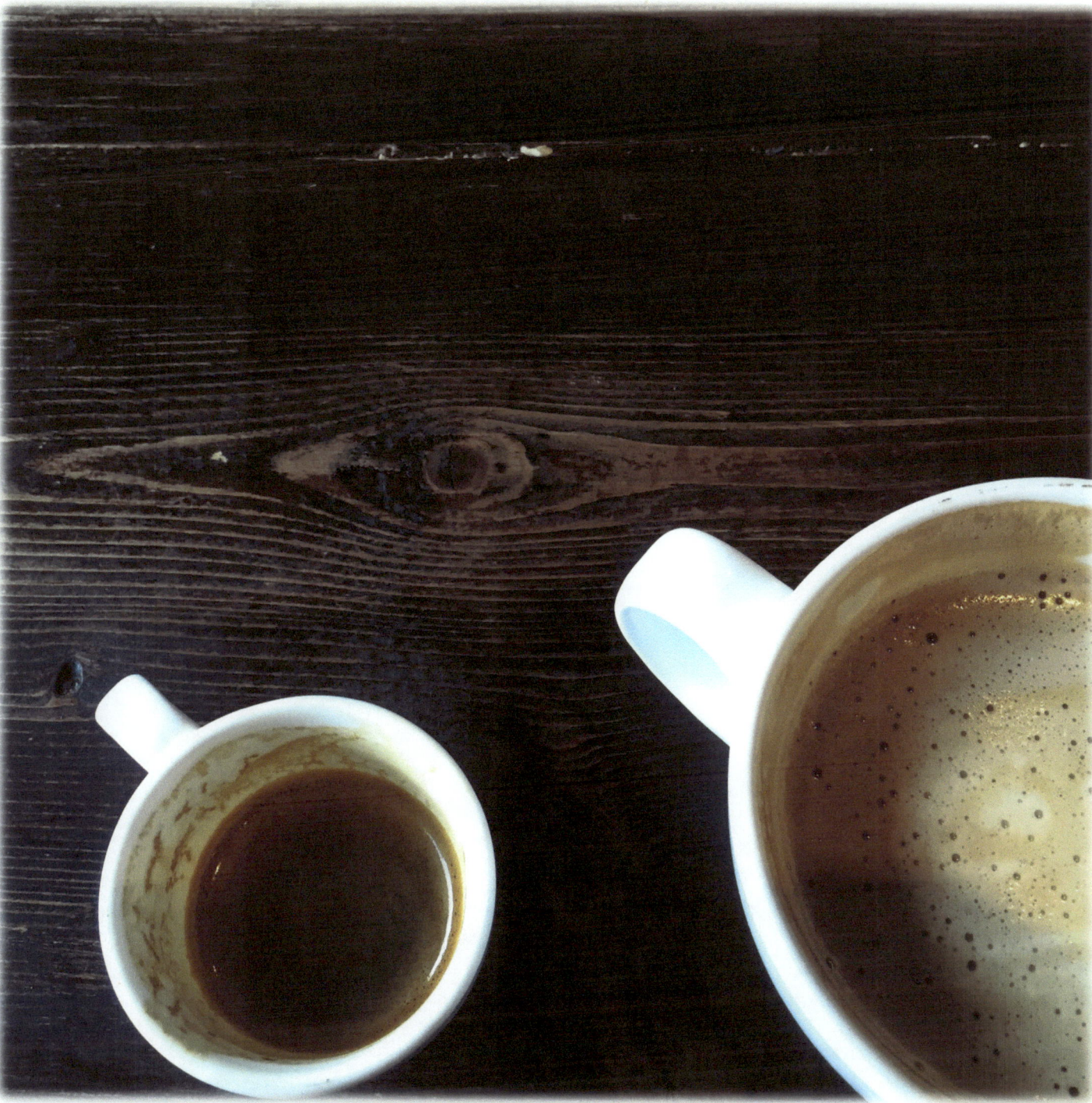

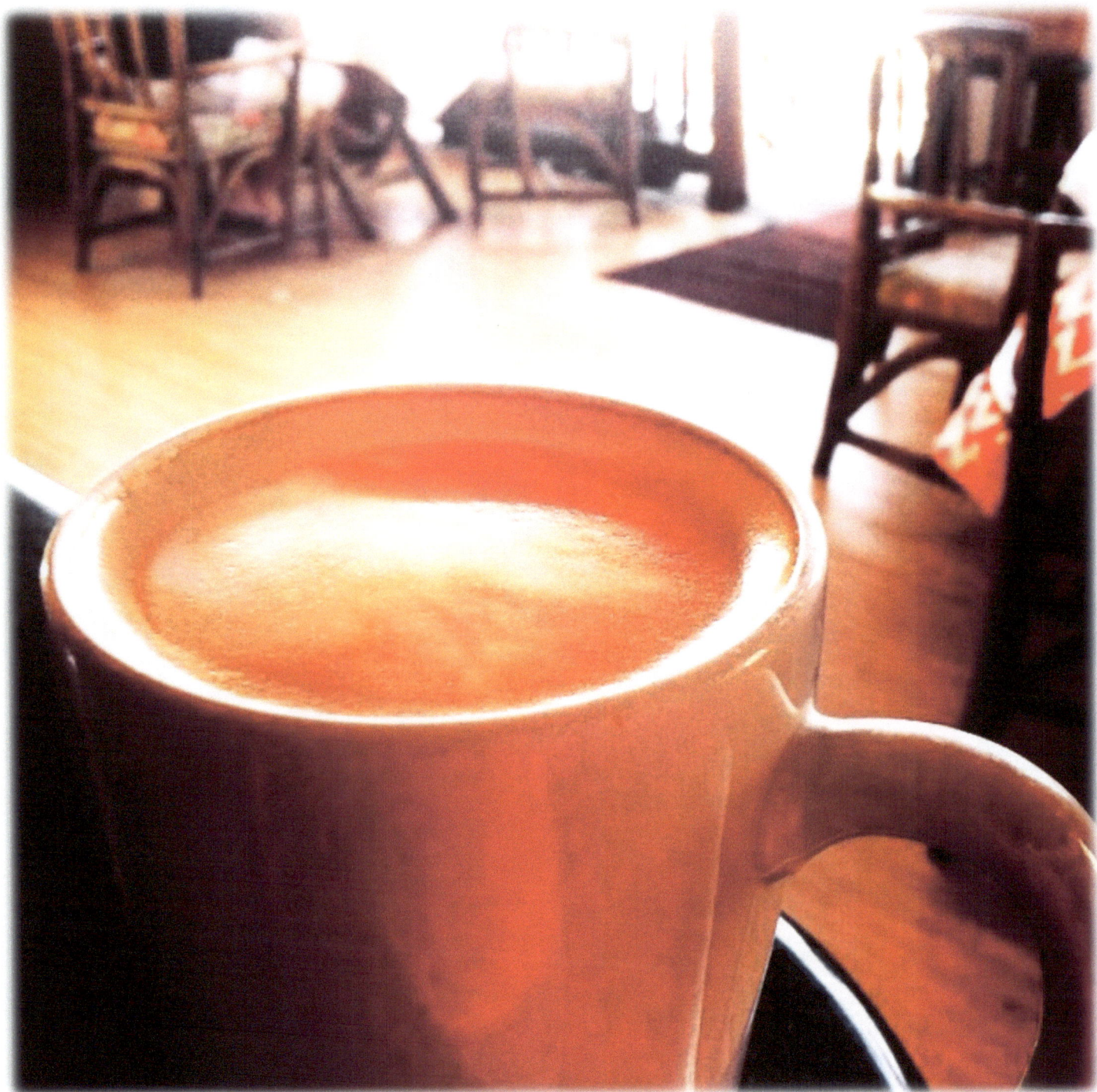

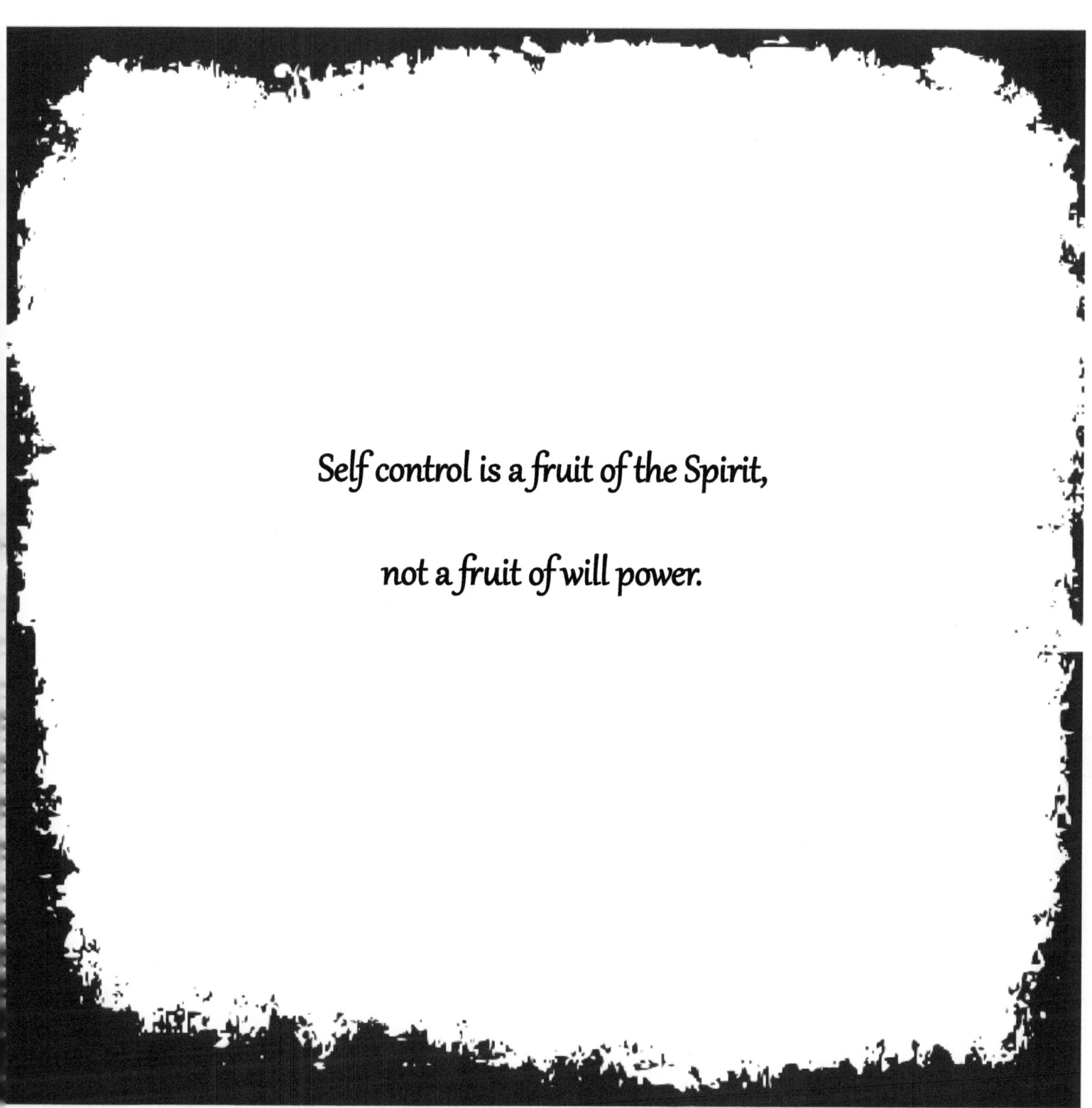

Self control is a fruit of the Spirit,

not a fruit of will power.

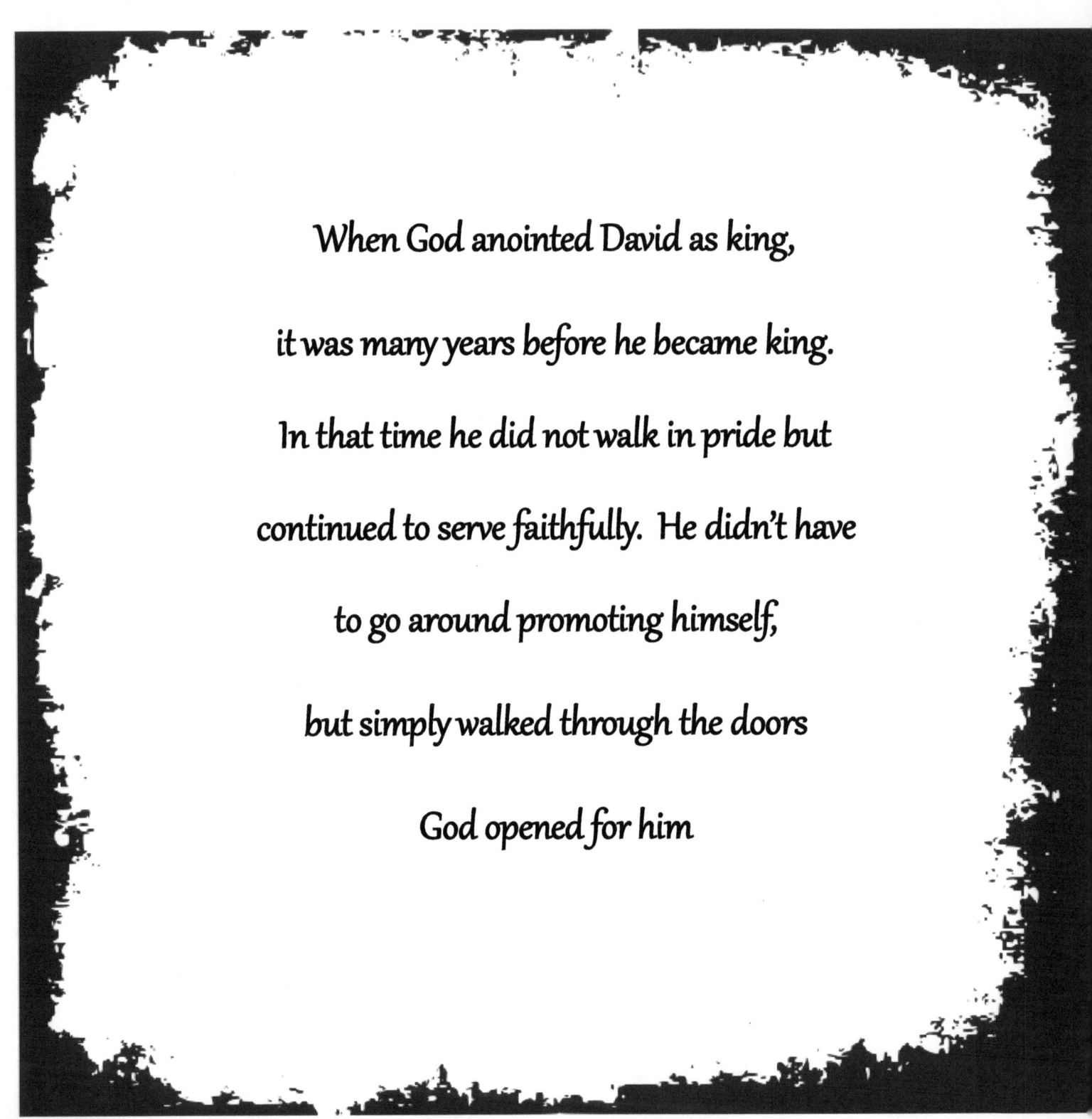

When God anointed David as king,

it was many years before he became king.

In that time he did not walk in pride but

continued to serve faithfully. He didn't have

to go around promoting himself,

but simply walked through the doors

God opened for him

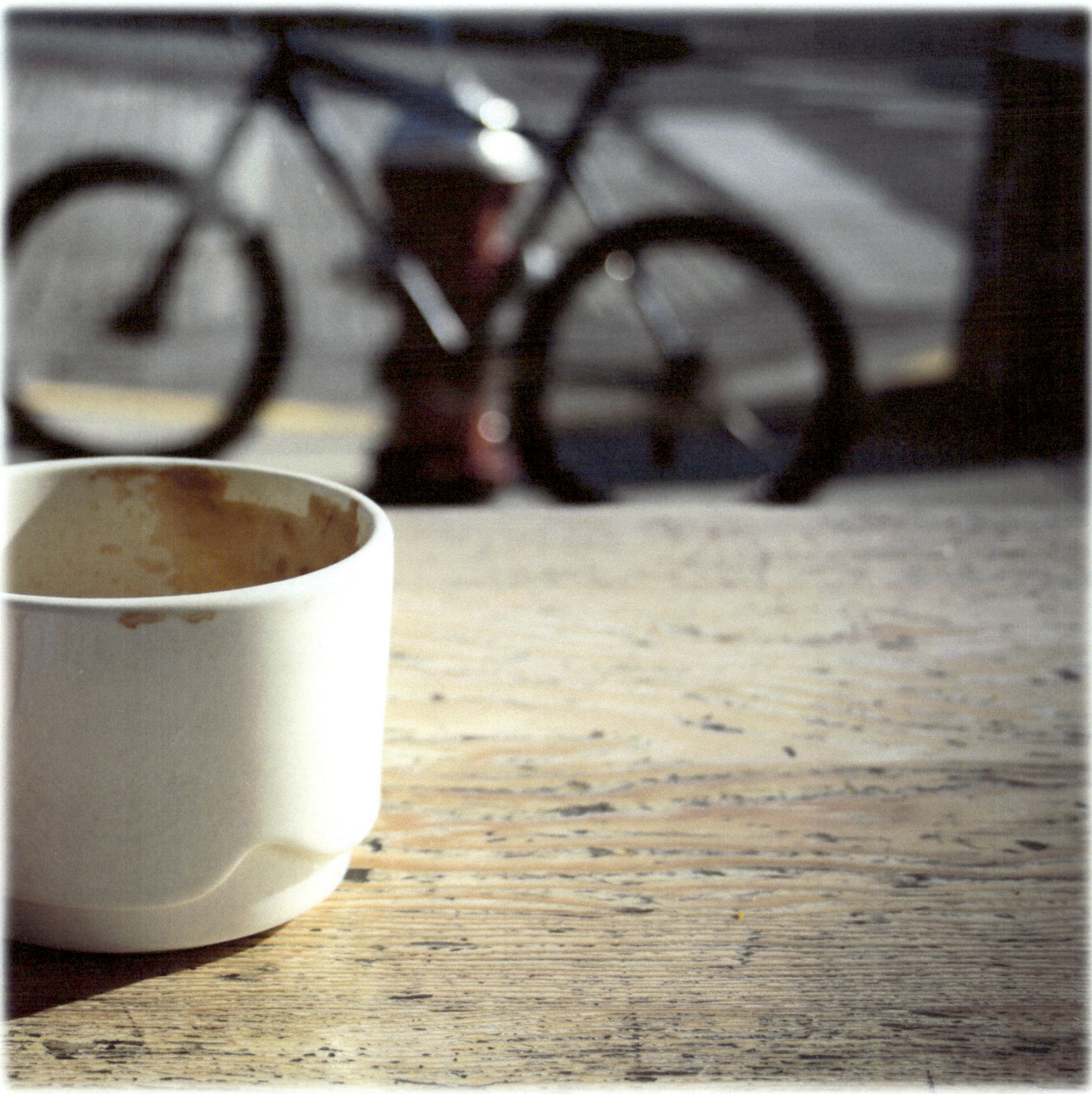

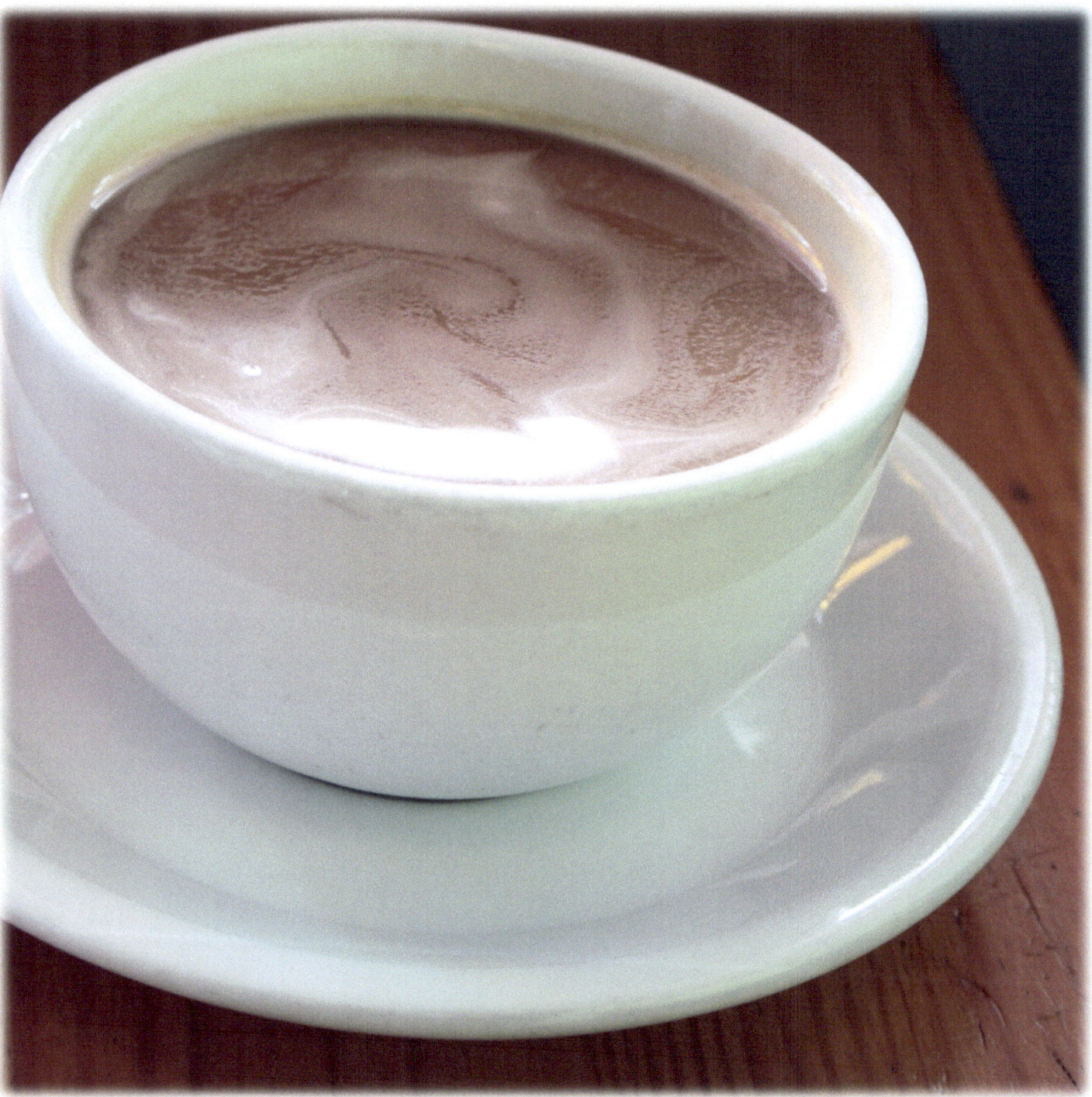

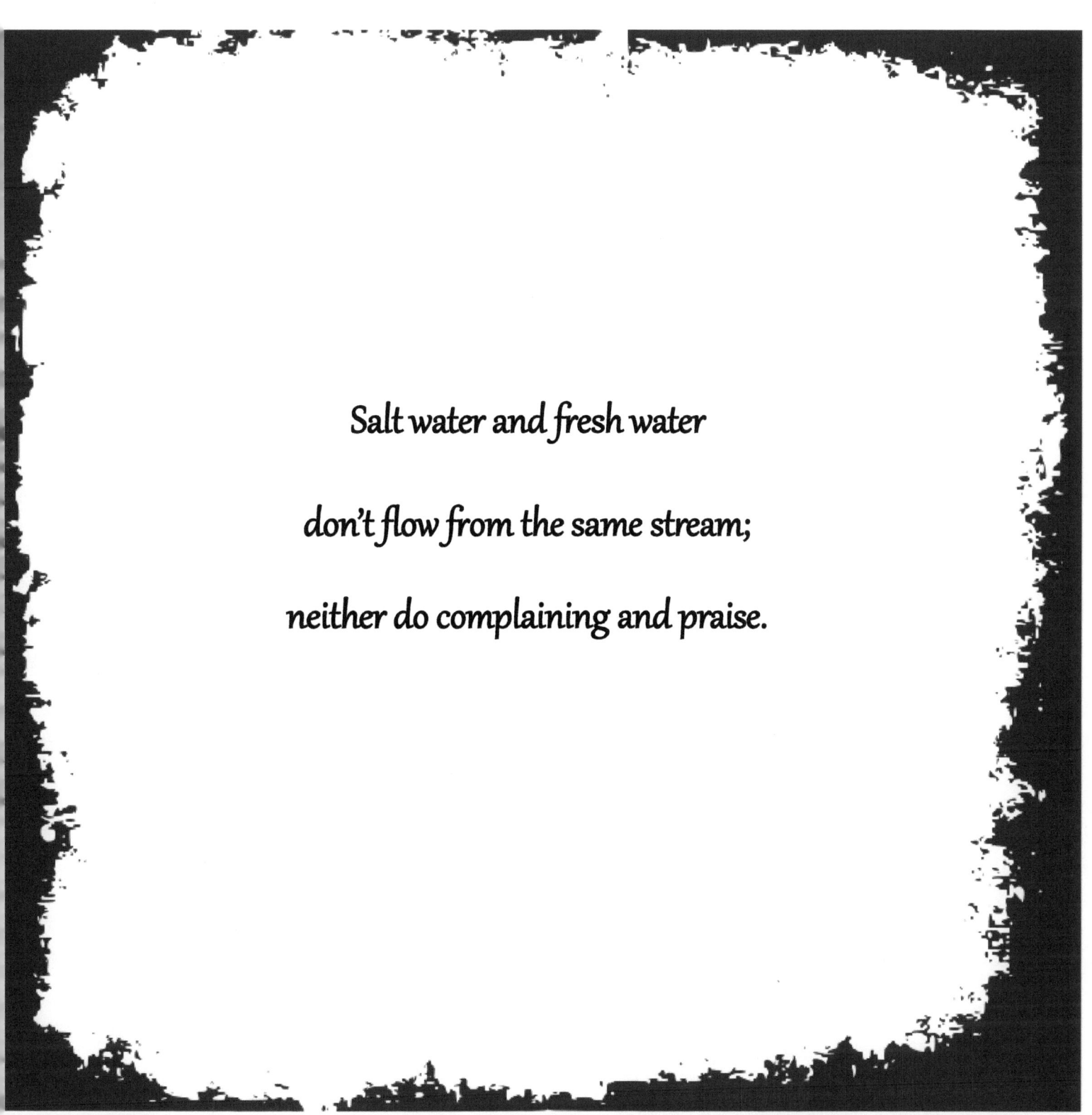

Salt water and fresh water

don't flow from the same stream;

neither do complaining and praise.

What if God wants to heal you but instead

of instantly, he wants to take you through a

process of healing so he can re-shape your

identity to what he originally had in mind

when he designed you?

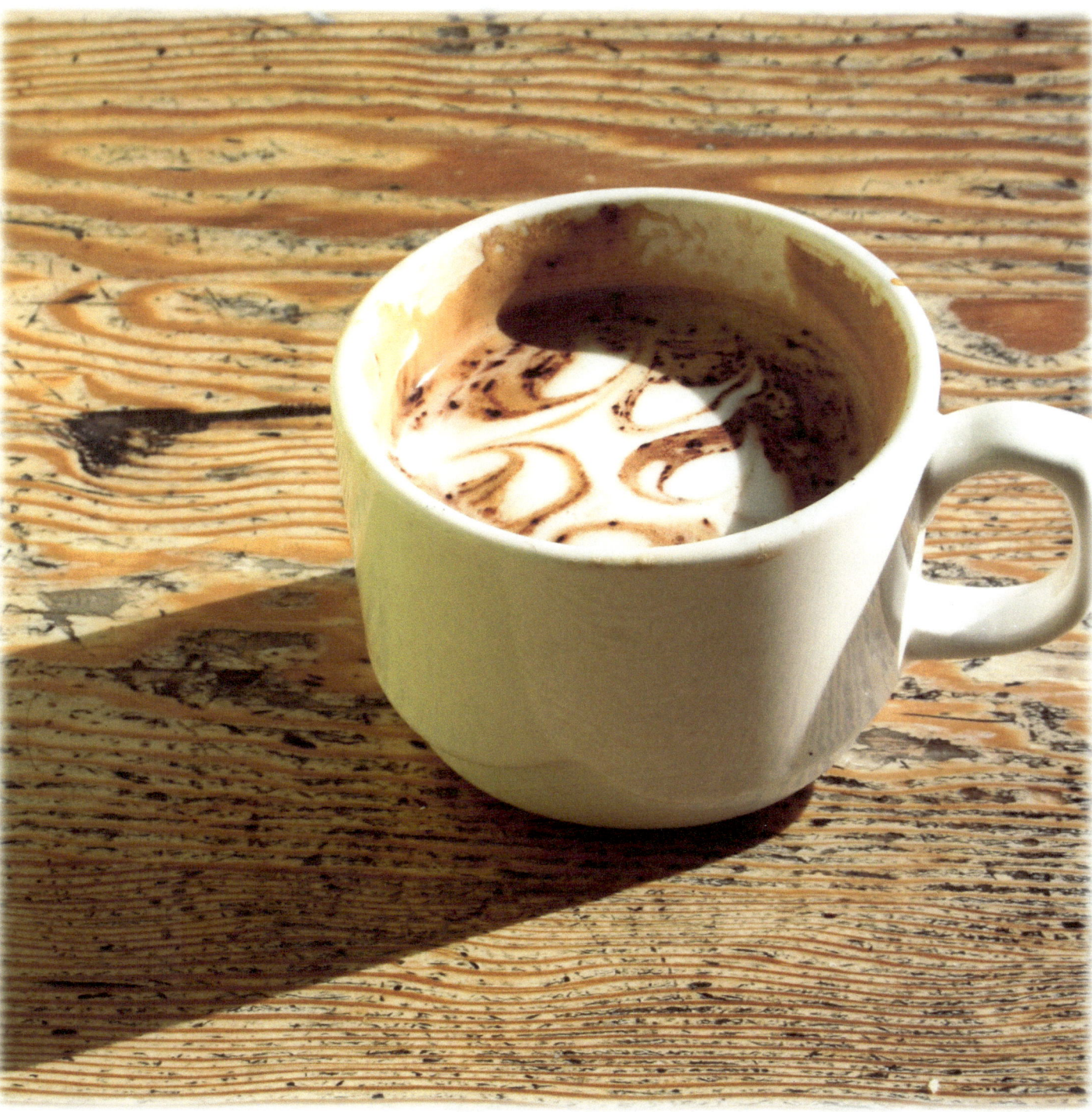

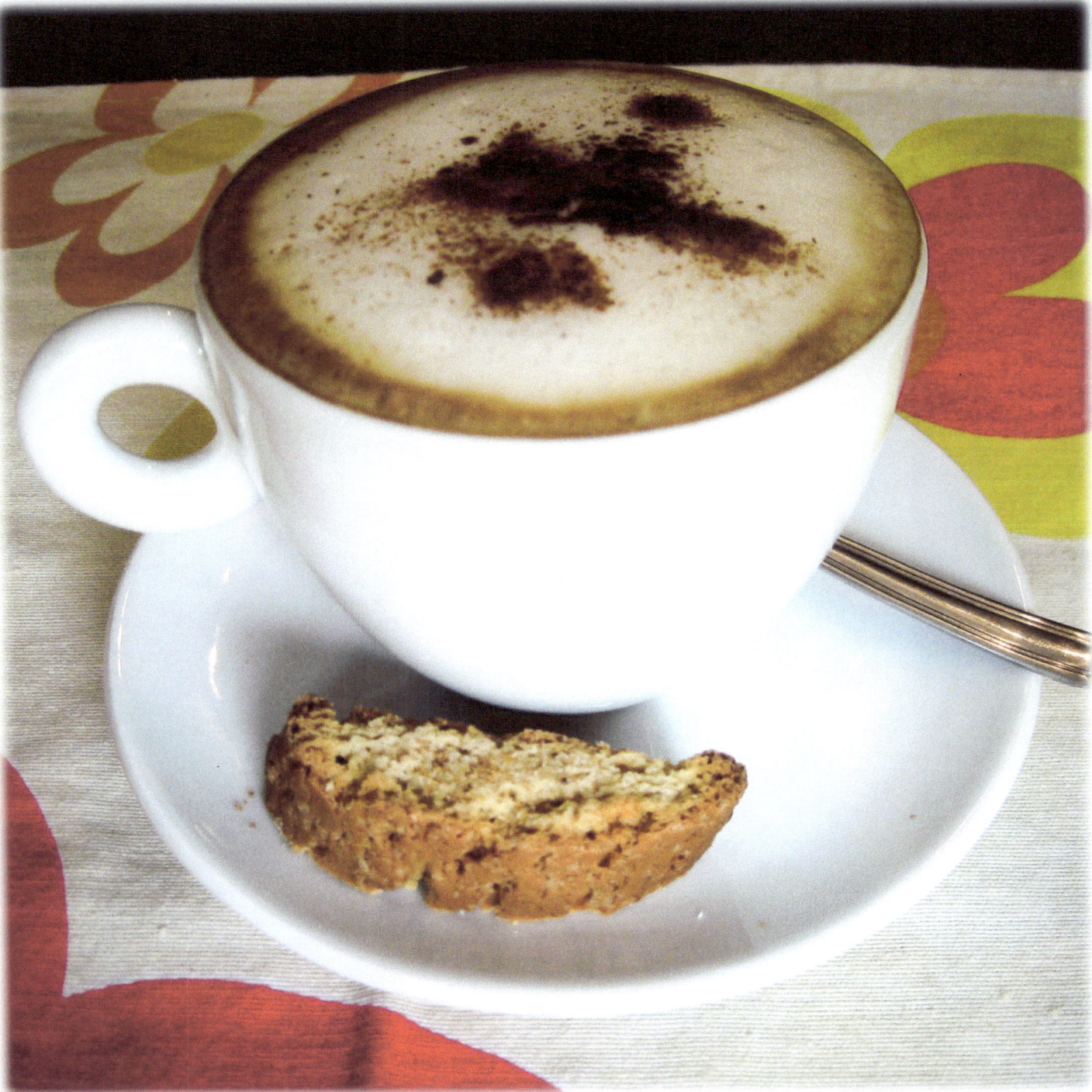

Since actions speak louder

than words, let's think about how

our actions are preaching!

God doesn't give you empty compliments.

He speaks truth directly to your heart.

Spend time with God. Just be.

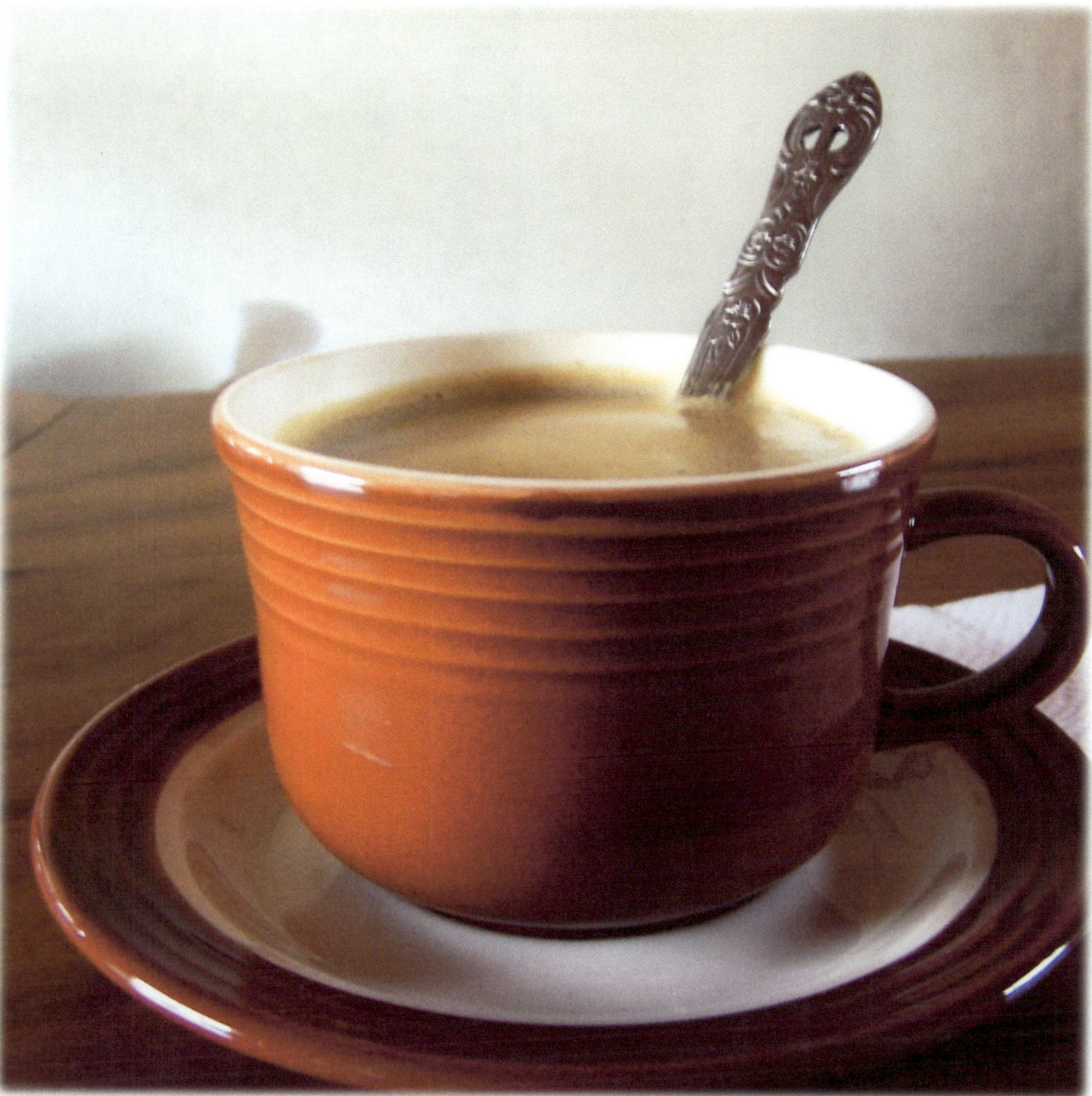

All photographs by

SONLIT Photography©

In collaboration with

Julieanne Marie Music

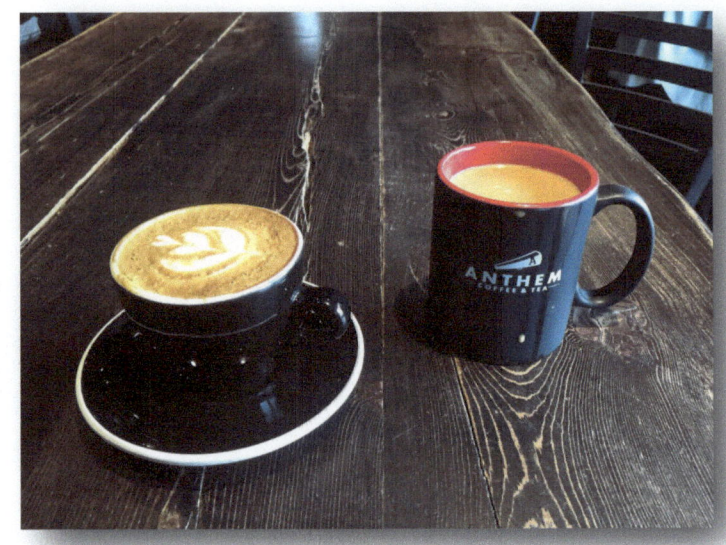

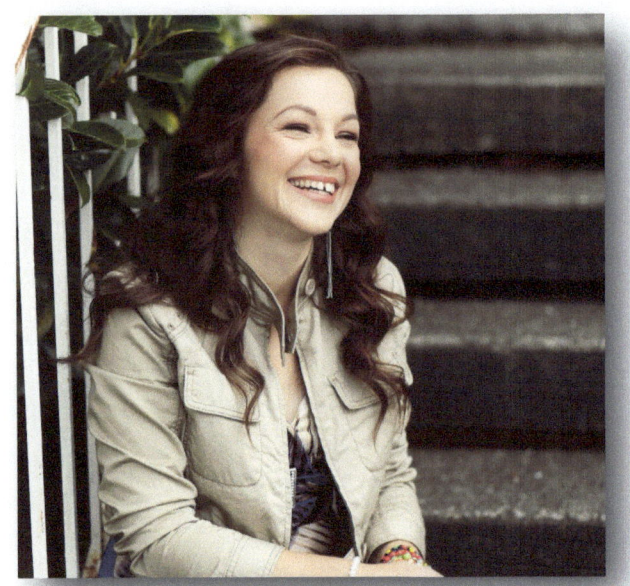

Be sure and visit Julieanne's

favorite coffee shops and

check out her newest music online!

@JulieanneMarieM

—- Julieanne Marie —-

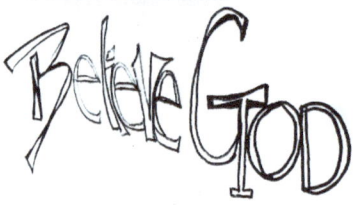

Remember God loves you.

www.ingramcontent.com/pod-product-compliance
Lightning Source LLC
Chambersburg PA
CBHW050818180526
45159CB00004B/1709